IN THE HEART
OR IN THE HEAD

IN THE HEART
OR IN THE HEAD

An Essay in Time Travel

GEORGE TURNER

Tell me where is fancy bred,
Or in the heart or in the head?
How begot, how nourished?
        Shakespeare, *Merchant of Venice,* III, ii

NORSTRILIA PRESS

Published by
Norstrilia Press
PO Box 91
Carlton, Victoria 3053
Australia

First published 1984

Published with the assistance of
the Literature Board of the Australia Council.

ISBN 0 909106 14 2

Typeset by Norstrilia Press.
Printed by Globe Press, Brunswick.

For BRUCE GILLESPIE, who asked for it,
and for those other curious folk who
simply wanted to know.

ACKNOWLEDGEMENTS

My thanks are due to:

John Foyster for his advice on the earlier chapters in the draft manuscript. The advice was taken.

John Bangsund for his editing and his patience with my carelessness.

Yvonne Rousseau for rescuing my memory from a disastrous gaffe.

The Literature Board of the Australia Council for financial support of the writing and publishing of this book.

CONTENTS

1
Why, Wherefore?

This book was simple in conception but its growth has been complex and difficult. I intended little more than a light-hearted account of myself and modern science fiction growing up together in a loose friendship until, at the age of sixty-two, I finally declared allegiance by producing a science fiction novel. The connecting thread throughout was to have been a question: Why, in his sixties, should a staidly respectable writer with half a dozen 'mainstream' novels behind him kick over his Australian-tradition traces and turn to science fiction, that most suspect of escapist genres?

The short answer could have been that it was inevitable from the moment of my encounter with Lewis Carroll at the age of three—inbuilt predilection recognizing destiny. But the short answer omits all the passions, strayings and estrangements by the way; also it raises the further question of what Lewis Carroll has to do with science fiction. And another as to how we managed to meet so early in my life.

The last question finally determined the content when I fell prey to memory, an unfair trap for one who had paid little attention to his past, preferring to let it lie where it fell on the rubbish tip of years. Memory and its forgetful uncertainties, working together, created a need to know, to force time to disgorge. A simple tale of childish enchantment flowering in an ageing man's pleasure became a search for the lost child.

Not every product of the hunt is recorded here. I am

a novelist at heart, not a biographer or a burden-shrugging confesser, so whole areas of the past have been chopped away and discarded because they do not bear directly on my theme. My years with the Commonwealth Employment Service, with the textile trade and in the brewery would make long chapters of human goodness, wickedness and fallibility, but they are off the point. The six traumatic war years become a chapter mainly of rumination, because the personal adventures are rarely relevant. My love life—poor, straggling thing—might have been ignored altogether had I not come to an episode of black comedy that changed my whole existence and could not be omitted; with no willingness on my part, in it went. (Setting down villainies is much easier than admitting stupidities.)

About two-thirds of the way through, the book ceases to be autobiographical save in short bursts updating the passage of time; it begins to talk about the carnival-coloured world-within-this-world of science fiction fandom, that most smoothly disorganized of subcultures, then about the business of writing and publishing in the antic genre world, and finally about science fiction itself, what it is and does and seeks to achieve.

It can't be pretended that these things matter as Shakespeare matters, or Einstein or Beethoven, but they have a real and pervasive importance and may come to have more. The justification for that statement is short, but it requires preparation, and it will have to wait two hundred pages or so until we are both ready for it.

It is a silly truth that very few people outside of a devoted readership know much about science fiction, and that what they do know is conditioned by films like *Star Wars* and *The Thing* (entertaining and harmless in themselves, but unimportant), television serials aimed quite properly at ten-year-olds (I don't think *Blake's Seven* could harm anyone), and the violently stupid covers of paperback novels, designed to claim the attention of the middle-aged ten-year-old.

That behind all this simplemindedness stands some solid intellectual responsibility and literary achievement, built up over decades of slogging against the current of rubbish, is not widely enough known.

The various critical areas have in recent years come to terms with the idea that a class of science fiction exists that should be taken seriously, and are treating the genre reasonably in review and criticism, but the magazine sections of newspapers are read by the already converted and the literary periodicals do not address a wide general public. All the friendly criticism in the language cannot counter the genial contempt engendered in the responsible mind by a ruthless commercial exploitation pandering to the lowest idiot denominator.

This is unfortunate, not only because too many remain ignorant of what a thoughtful science fiction has to say about today as well as tomorrow, but also because they remain ignorant of just how deeply the *spirit* of science fiction has penetrated their daily lives and swayed their thoughts and actions. Science fiction, existing in an unbridled intellectual extravagance because it answers extravagant popular needs, pervades every cultural activity, from common speech to poetry and the jargon of politicians, from rock music to opera, from real science to occultism and the horror film, from advertising art to gallery art, from architecture and sculpture to the design of children's toys.

That is what much of this book is about.

It is also about being just another novelist in a profession, and a world, geared to superstardom.

3

PART ONE
PARALLEL LIVES

2a
Books and Sorceries

Memory is not enough and I have never been a journal keeper. The past continually vanishes from recollection, uninteresting times because they are not worth revisiting, darker passages because the censor that keeps the unbearable under control has relegated them to oubliettes of repression. What remains is subject to the erosion of time and the distortions of viewpoint and, at least in the maternal branch of my family, to a compulsion to embroider until simple truth is submerged in a good story. Soon the good story becomes truth and no-one admits to remembering differently.

So we will be afloat on seas of probability—but this, in the world of a science fiction writer, or in the world of a mathematician or a physicist for that matter, is a normal and rational situation.

Relativity of truth asserts itself from the moment of birth. Though West Australian, I was actually born in a Melbourne suburb: the parental home was in Kalgoorlie, but since my mother bore me while on a visit to Victoria, it has always seemed too much of a quibble to explain dual statehood to anyone who asks.

We lived on the goldfields, half-way between Kalgoorlie and Boulder, fairly in the middle of the great mining strip, though that section was by then worked out and silent. Beside the house a red poppet-head rose to the sky in steps and landings; behind us yawned a vast, unfenced open-cut mine, still scratched at by fossickers. The open-cut fascinated me, forbidden because of its fencelessness; from its rough rim I could gaze down and down into the rock-tumbled heart of the world, and fancy what strangeness lurked.

A visit after half a century showed the poppet-head as a poor thing to eyes grown indifferent to the uprush of cities, and the open-cut a large but unimpressive hole in the ground. The two realities coexist, but it is the childhood memory that dominates with its images imprinted in the age of wonderment; poppet-head and open-cut are for ever vast. Romance 'recollected in tranquillity' defies facts.

The house sat solitary in an acre of ground, the nearest neighbour a quarter mile beyond the open-cut, an enormous distance to a child's eye. It was verandahed back and front against early and late sunlight (for Kalgoorlie summers can be ferocious) and locked in by trellises of purple, paper-flowered virginia creeper and sweet yellow honeysuckle. Down one side grew a vegetable garden, where pea vines climbed wires and stakes to wave their tendrils higher than my parents' heads.

Do I really remember that? Perhaps not, but an old sepia photograph insists that it was so.

In the paddock of a back yard—an acre is empire-sized when you are young enough—were a hen run, a pigeon loft, a duck pen and a huge firewood pile, which was my favourite playground. (In Kalgoorlie in the 1920s we had wood stoves, and kitchens were hell-holes.) There was also, in the furthest north-eastern corner, an outdoor dunny—no other word fits those sweatboxes—wherein a clamped-down lid and lashings of turpentine defeated neither smell nor flies. It was, for very short legs, too far away for the taken-unaware, so I deposited my tokens in secret but nearer places—usually discovered within minutes. Essie, the maid, would not tell on me, but the simple, retarded outside man, Jack, would bellow 'Shit, shit, shit!' in mixed malice and glee until my mother arrived bearing punishment, the featherless end of a feather duster.

Life was adventurous but unshared; in my empire I played alone.

I had a brother, Frank, fourteen years older and attending

Melbourne Grammar eighteen hundred miles away. It was an exile demanded by the cultural snobbery of the time. The sons of the well-off could not easily be entered for Eton or Winchester (it took more than money to power that leap) but they could be sent to the swankier Australian boarding schools, and were. A local education lacked status in Kalgoorlie 'society', and my mother does seem to have had some social position. My father was a mines accountant, which made the Turners Somebody on the Golden Mile, and Ethel Turner* was not one to miss out on being Somebody to the hilt. Side effects of social position were for brother Frank exile to distant Melbourne and for her the alienation of her eldest son. The drawing of morals may be left to the uninvolved.

Social position provided no companionship for a small boy. The perfunctory petting of the town dames at my mother's 'afternoons' was no substitute. The nearest of these lived beyond the open-cut, and venturing round that dangerous deep brought quick punishment. During my first six years I had only the very occasional company of another child; I am told that when at these rare meetings I was urged to play with strange children I would either hit them or burst into tears.

I learned self-sufficiency, accepting company only on my own terms, making friends with reluctance and then treating them with brusqueness or outright rudeness when I wished them elsewhere. Later regrets cut no ice with them and drew no tears from me.

Sixty years on, it still happens.

I had a dog. He was small and grey and hairy and produced a bright pink erection when I patted his tummy. He was my beloved and only friend—and I feel guilty because I can't remember his name. He did not last long, and the manner of his passing is clearer to me than the short joy of his life.

He died by pointless accident. One of the few pleasures my father actively shared with me was an evening climb to the second stage of the poppet-head, to gaze over miles of countryside where the towns of Boulder and Kalgoorlie

---

* No, not the children's writer of that name.

balanced either hand, and catch the sundown breeze. It was a perilous climb, because the steps were treads only, with no risers in the spaces between; my father would hold my hand all the way. One evening the dog followed us up and fell through the steps to break his back on a rusting boiler twenty feet below.

This is, I think, my first floodlit true memory; it was my first acquaintance with death.

It became, when we returned home, an acquaintance with life, which can be infinitely more terrible. My mother stormed from room to room, abusing my father for what she swore was criminal carelessness, while he pleaded 'But my dear Etta' and got no further. It was a dark moment, with the quality of bleakness whose meaning becomes clear only after years have passed. I don't recall the accusations, only the storm of words at the heart of them and the pre-defeated protest, 'But my dear Etta'.

My father was fifty-one when I was born and my mother about thirty-five; since Frank was already fourteen the reasonable conclusion is that somebody was careless. Whatever the fact, my mother had the guardian-tigress attitude towards her young, and my father was allowed little say in discipline or rearing. I have this on the authority of uncles and aunts, of whom there were great numbers, hangovers of the late Victorian era of determined fruitfulness. He was permitted access only under supervision and controlled conditions.

He was a small, fat man. The only photograph I have seen, that with the towering pea vines, shadows his face too heavily to show personality or stir recognition. I know that he stood only five feet and half an inch, a half inch shorter than my mother, that he was bald at twenty, that he was a Baptist, was educated at Wesley College in Melbourne and sang a high tenor in some church choir. My mother claimed, after the inevitable catastrophe, that he was a drunk and a skirt-chaser, but I soon found that her opinions of anything and anybody were extreme, biased and unreliable. I think she gave him a rough time of it. There are flashes of other rows after the first, but no flash of all three of us ever doing something enjoyable together.

Yet it was he who with a single beneficence influenced my future more than did my mother in thirty years of sullen skirmishing. She left only scars, but he read *Alice in Wonderland* to me.

In the Kalgoorlie house was a smallish room between the dining-room and the kitchen called, in proper social usage, the Breakfast Room; it was in fact the room in which we did most of our daily living. In 1919 one did not use the dining-room save on social occasions, when it assumed capitals as the Dining Room; between times it was preserved in a splendour of woodwork and leather, with glassware glistening and untouchable in display cases. When not on public view we huddled in the all-purpose breakfast room (without capitals), and it was there that my father lifted me to his lap and into the enchantment of the most magical of all books.

It seems that when he had finished it in a one-chapter-a-night ritual, I demanded that he at once begin again. And so he did—and again, so the family legend runs, and then again. The legend credits me with learning the book by heart and 'reading' it aloud to audiences who presumably oohed and aahed in accesses of boredom, even with the showman touch of turning the pages at the correct words. Turner legend is brittle stuff, enriched by many a lively flourish but cavalier with fact.

Behind this legend lies the truth of an influence that has lasted all my life. *Alice* set me on paths that have been strayed from but never forsaken.

For good or evil, particular books have influenced my life. Joy cannot be understood without an apprehension of misery, so another book counterbalanced *Alice* with a monster whose grip also endured.

May Gibbs published *Snugglepot and Cuddlepie* in 1918; it captivated me with its illustrations when it was read to me soon after *Alice*. Its supersweetness seems too coy for the modern child but it still appears in the bookshops at Christmas, and in that innocent day I loved the Gumnut

11

Babies in the colourful pictures. But I feared their enemy, the Banksia Man.

The Banksia Man was the villain, a terror of matted hair and malice in endless pursuit. May Gibbs's illustration—the bushy cob of the banksia tree with eyes glaring from the tangle as it ran on knotty legs—was my vision of horror and evil. It haunted my dreams; for a shameful number of years I feared the dark and the lurking beast.

One day—I would have been about four—my mother sat combing her hair while I watched; it was a daily ritual. In the fashion of the time her hair fell waist-length—thick and brown, it covered her head and shoulders, tumbling and concealing to make a mystery of her face.

This day was different from all others. Perhaps we were making a game of her hiding behind her hair, or perhaps I was unwontedly quiet; whatever the reason, suddenly she swept the tumble aside and her dark eyes glared out while she growled in pretended menace.

In a shock of knowledge, fiction and reality met. I saw the Banksia Man alive behind my mother's hair. I had no words to explain my screaming or she the secret knowledge to do more than comfort without comprehending. It was a cruelty of blind chance, but the sudden gap between us was never bridged.

Years later, in the Melbourne Botanical Gardens, I at last saw a living banksia tree with its conelike flowers of bundled, curly hair; it is not a repulsive thing, just quaint and harmless. Nightmares retreated before the uninteresting reality, but the barrier raised in a moment of love had been fixed for ever. To a very small child there is no such thing as a *token* terror.

Kalgoorlie was a long time ago; its remains are a dead dog, parental brawling, a book of disturbing influence and another of endless charm.

Of these death is the least interesting. Thomas Mann noted in *The Magic Mountain* that 'A man's dying is more the survivors' affair than his own'; the deaths of others can spark emotional loss, or relief (when truth is told), and nearly always represent a nuisance in practical terms; one's own death, being simply an end of participation, is by virtue of the fact beyond fussing over. Having observed the passage into impersonal stillness, I have found little in it to require contemplation. The *way* of it, perhaps—but pain and fear are other matters.

The parental brawling is gone along with the brawlers; if its effects persist, that cannot be helped, but the fact is dustily antique. So also with the Banksia Man; he did his damage and was abandoned.

But *Alice* has never been altogether away from me, only neglected a little, to return at last in force. She deserves closer attention.

2b

Behind the Sorcerer's Mask

Alice in Wonderland tapped an ecstasy of visions as real as the 'real' world. They existed in a different kind of reality but needed no explaining. What the mind perceived *was*. I talked with the White Rabbit in our garden. Often.

The invisible playmate is a psychiatric commonplace; it is his persistence into maturity that troubles common sense. It was this innocent confusion of perceptions that led at last to science fiction (which is never innocent), though by a tortuous and often obscure track.

In these days of pragmatism masquerading as political philosophy, the Carrollian method of seizing the world by the scruff of its illusions may make a better recipe for understanding it than mulling over its dreary record of blood and self-deception. Writing science fiction is that part of the seizing which records and puzzles over paradox and inconsistency in the hope of seeing a little—however little—more clearly. The connection with *Alice* may not be immediately obvious, but Carroll would have spotted it at once.

The acceptance of *Alice* as a timeless book for children confirms success on the obvious plane but obscures the subtextual nature of the creation, and it is there that the connection lies. The humour of *Alice* is expressed super-ficially in the pointing of paradox and absurdity, a mode that George Bernard Shaw ground to needle sharpness in plays that began to appear while Carroll still lived. Shaw's ferocious wit would have horrified the gentle Charles Dodgson, yet it was a wit founded like his own on the recognition of incongruities as comments on life.

14

Dodgson/Carroll—the mathematician and the wit together make a man—did not write science fiction;* nor did he, in the strictest sense, write what is vaguely termed 'fantasy'. Fantasy in its pure form depends on the denial of physical likelihood or even possibility. An early fantasist could have been the cave man who fancied his dinner dropping dead at his feet to save him the chore of hunting it. This is the denial expressed in dreams, those symbolic creations which bypass all limitations of reality to come at once to their psychological point.

Carroll's flights of fancy were rarely dreamlike, and he was not the man to provide a fancy-creature with red eyes simply because red eyes may symbolize a blazing nastiness; he required more than dream and symbol. Nor were his flights narrative conveniences, as in the introduction of a magic wand simply to get characters out of a dilemma; for Carroll both the wand and the dilemma would have had to be representations of the desperately uncertain nature of the universe. Behind each of his 'fantasies' lurked the destructuring mind of an anarchic philosopher-mathematician. He did not fantasize; he extrapolated received knowledge and theory to points beyond the edge of reason.

Here, in Chapter 2 of *Alice*, is the Carrollian mind at work (Alice is speaking): 'Let me see: four times five is twelve, and four times six is thirteen, and four times seven is—oh dear! I shall never get to twenty at that rate!'

Just a little nonsense to make the children giggle? Well, yes—but *why* will she never get to twenty?

Think of this: In 1865, when *Alice* was published, the arithmetic tables were commonly learned by chanting a litany in class: 'two times two is four, three times two is six' and so on, ending at 'twelve times twelve'. (Sixty years later we were still at it; surely education has by now come up with something less deadening.) Alice's progression—

---

* Shaw found the apparatus of science fiction to hand for the writing of his 'metabiological pentateuch', *Back to Methuselah*. It was an apparatus ready-made for the expression of that play's ideas, and it is precisely the expression of ideas that is the concern of the properly responsible science fiction writer today.

4 x 5 = 12, 4 x 6 = 13, 4 x 7 = 14—could never 'get to twenty' because 4 x 13 would be twenty, and everybody knows that the multiplication table stops at 'times twelve'. Thirteen times anything is toil for pencil and paper and knotted brow.

Behind the nonsense was a mathematician's joke about the mutability of number systems and an educationist's passing tilt at the teaching method. No 'fantasy' here, only accepted reality transmuted into the nonsense he perceived inherent in it.

Such logical joking is the backbone of Carroll's humour, not all of it mathematical. The Red King's dream sequence in *Through the Looking Glass*, for instance, is an undisguised discussion of Berkeleian reality, with Tweedledum and Tweedledee arguing the Bishop's case while Alice stands stoutly for materialism. The child skips through it as comic cross-talk but the adult, resampling his childhood, may be jolted into realizing that in this charming entertainment his very existence is sneakily held up for questioning.*

The Alice books are the agile games of a mind at play with the universe. The reasonably sensitive adult reader perceives the Carrollian manipulations in some fashion, if rarely with full understanding; he recognizes disturbingly not only the stuff of dreams but the presence of a structure behind it, immanent, pervasive, but eluding easy comprehension.

Here the relationship with science fiction emerges. The Alice books are absurdist fun-poking of the kind that such playwrights as Orton and Ionesco have employed (though their intentions, like Shaw's, were not merely to amuse), and that many science fiction writers have used often and well and by no means always in simple fun. Bernard

* I claim no expertise in Carroll exegesis. My two examples, with many others, will be found in *The Annotated Alice*, edited by the science journalist Martin Gardner for Clarkson & Potter in the USA and Penguin Books in England. Many psychological analyses of the Alice books and their author are available but, unlike Gardner's book, they add little to the reader's enjoyment; most have theoretical axes, predominantly Freudian, to grind, whereas Gardner's explorations are founded solidly on the texts of the books.

Wolfe's *Limbo* and Anthony Burgess's *A Clockwork Orange* turned it into a weapon of menace and warning. But they, of course, are known as 'mainstream' writers, not to be confused with genre sensationalists. (We will consider that idiotic distinction later in the book.) If the names of receivedly 'science fictional' authors are required to make the point, I suggest for attention some earnest, honourable and very competent modern genre writers: John Sladek, Michael Moorcock and R. A. Lafferty have used the method with gaiety, J. G. Ballard has bypassed humour for less happy ponderings, and Thomas M. Disch has wept outright over the ruins.

On second thought, none of those five would care to be categorized as a genre writer of science fiction, but the taxonomic desperation of publishers, critics and readers jams the ill-fitting cap on their work. However, it is too soon to begin arguing that worthwhile science fiction obeys no genre rules and fits no pigeonholes. Later, later . . .

At this point the reader is entitled to protest that, yes, he sees after a fashion what I am driving at, that Carroll and Ionesco and the science fiction writers use similar techniques for commenting on the world, but, well, he has seen 'science fiction' lining the newsagent's paperback racks, and what has all this talk to do with that kind of thing? Where, in Carroll and Orton and Shaw and Ballard and the rest, are the death rays, space cruisers, telepaths, lecherous monsters and alien planets of doom?

They certainly are not in Carroll *et al.,* and in this book we will not be much interested in their gaudy existence. They represent science fiction about as well as a Mickey Spillane thriller represents the fictional dissection of the criminal mind whose great genius was Dostoyevsky.

We are in pursuit of the real thing, not the slap-happy spin-offs of popular acclaim.

That surely is an admirable and literate attitude, but what is this 'real thing'? How can it be recognized on the bookseller's shelf, where even the best quality science fiction wears a jacket designed to sell it at the lowest common denominator of public appeal?

17

There are no easy answers to those questions. The first, begging a definition of the genre, has never been settled by writers, readers or interested academics, and the second may defeat the most experienced forager. Still, useful if incomplete answers are possible. Call them guidelines. To arrive at them we will have to move through some six thousand years of literary experience, seeking the seed that grew into science fiction. Once found, it will be possible to see what, if anything, sets it apart from other fiction and to provide an answer, however tentative, to the question of what science fiction is. Only then will it be possible to consider matters of quality, usefulness and critical discussion.

It will be a longish journey and, I think, an interesting one, with some nosing into curious corners.

But first, back to the small boy stumbling through the tears and wonders of a life in the making.

3a

What We Were,
Where We Came From

My father's job, the snob-factor that gave us a little local clout, was his and our downfall. What my mother told me of it long afterwards was no doubt true in essence but there must have been strains and conflicts of which she said nothing. My father, as a mines staff employee, was not permitted to operate on the stock market, presumably because as an accountant he had access to privileged information. 'But', said my mother, 'they all did it.' Perhaps they did. *He* was caught at it.

Loss of his job was only the doorknock of disaster, announcing the Income Tax assessors and humiliating disclosures covering years. They broke him financially. Add that he at once became unemployable in a one-business town and the catastrophe became total.

According to my mother—and I must stress the family penchant for legend building—Father had been drawing a salary of two thousand pounds a year. The figure, if correct, opens avenues of speculation. Forty pounds a week, when a day labourer would have been well paid at two pounds, seems an inordinate amount, though it may have been boosted to cover the confidential nature of the work and padded to compensate for the prohibition on side trading. It would be roughly equivalent to $60,000 a year today and one can only wonder why it was necessary to grub after more at the risk of losing it all. In very young innocence I asked my mother this question and got a stonewall reply: 'You wouldn't understand.'

In that day a child accepted this as a proper answer, indicative of mysteries of behaviour not to be broached until a time called 'years of discretion' had been reached. Parents used it unstintingly. The newly fashionable psychology had not penetrated country-town tea-parties and might have been pooh-poohed if it had; few would have wondered if unanswered questions might one day return in vengeance.

It did not pay to pursue you-wouldn't-understand queries—repetition brought anger without enlightenment—but later I constructed my own scenario of the crash, one centring on expenditure. Item, brother Frank a boarder at Melbourne Grammar; item, a second maid's room, kitchen and sewing-room built onto the house in 1921; item, rounds of hospitality wherein ladies strove to outdo, and in winter, costume balls for charity; item, my mother and myself spending summer months in Melbourne each year in refuge from the desert heat. Add outlays I could never be aware of and the sum speaks of wealthy living. (Was it this that gave him away?) Two thousand pounds a year was by no means great wealth—it was more than comfortable but less than regal.

I learned early who was head of the family, and she claimed never to have questioned the finances. 'That was your father's business.' ('Your father', never 'Edgar'.) Indeed she could add and subtract very well, but she was also socially ambitious and unable to bear the thought of being less than first among competing equals.

Which was the prodigal? Both? Not until my mother's death, a quarter of a century later, could I ask directly of her sister, my Aunt Linda: 'Whose fault?' She, out of her forty years of training in social diplomacy (of which more in its place), replied that 'Ethel did not reveal herself to anybody' and added: 'She believed what she wished to believe.'

It was as much as I could hope for.

The house was sold up. My mother brought me to Melbourne and rented a small flat in South Yarra; my father went in the opposite direction, to Perth, for 'business reasons' never explained. He was to join us in Melbourne in three months but did not. I never saw him again.

I was six years old.

As the months passed my mother's reserve exploded in

rage; she spoke of him as 'cowardly animal' and 'miserable skunk'. The words are memories, not hearsay.

For a while he sent money, then no more.

When it no longer mattered I asked Linda about that, too, again bluntly: 'Why did he desert us? Could he stand no more of her?'

Linda was loyal enough not to answer, honest enough not to contradict.

My mother's purgatory began. It was to last until she died in 1948.

From Frank she met the first rebuff for mistaken ambition, killing any hope of mending a fragmented family. He was just twenty, out of school with a first-class sporting record and not much else, and working as a salesman in an electrical goods store. The job meant in cash terms little more than he needed to stay decently alive; she knew he could not be a financial prop; what ground deep was that he had no desire to live with us, and he never did.

The years at Melbourne Grammar, designed to gain him a useful social footing, paid off in debased coin; he gained a footing of a sort but lost all sense of unity with the family that had exiled him at the age of twelve. Nor was there solace in the 'society' he had chosen: his circle was upper-middle-class South Yarra, second or third drawer as things then went, working for its living but conscious of superior education and the finer points of etiquette— a last remnant of Australia's imitation English, and failing fast. Still, he had learned something of social realities, enough to see clearly through the Turner pretensions and know us for an upstart pack whose chances had never existed.

There is time, while we are still in that short-lived flat existence, to see what manner of upstarts we were, where we came from and to what blind alleys we were headed.

Of my father's family I know only that there were many of them; they were people of hearsay whom, with one important exception, I never met. My mother's side was equally large and just as much animated by hearsay, but this was hearsay embellished by contact with the originals,

21

adorned with garrulous but magical reminiscence, mostly bogus, and electrified by spats of instant drama, also bogus, and directed to ends of one-upmanship or petty intrigue.

I must have met most of them during the summer jaunts to Victoria but they take on recollected flesh only in the Melbourne settlement of 1922.

We were all, excepting my Aunt Linda, just a little mad (not always amusingly) and Grandma Gill was the maddest, as unlikely a matriarch as ever failed to hold a family together; there's no reason to think she ever tried. With her the family distortions, fancies and concealments begin with the discreet suppression of all mention of Grandpa Gill. She never spoke of him but it was whispered that, having fathered ten children on her during breaks from other dalliance, he ran off to Brisbane with a Salvation Army lass. It could be true; it is the sort of anti-romantic skeleton for which our cupboards are built.

A search of public records might fill such gaps, but it seems hardly worth the trouble. We never formed a family in any close fashion; brothers, sisters and cousins exchanged visits and sometimes joined forces to keep Grandma's behaviour within bounds, but an air of duty accomplished hung over their meetings. It is not easy to believe that any of them cared a damn about the others; they rarely talked family because effectively there was no family. I was well into my teens when I heard—and not from my mother—that two other boys, Herbert and Eric, had been born to her and had died in infancy. She was a woman who had no luck—no luck at all.

Only Ellen Gill—flamboyant, predatory and loaded with cunning—could force them into defensive alliance. They would have liked to ignore and forget her, but ignoring Grandma was a high-risk procedure.

She lived, when I first remember her, in Carlton, in a terrace that no longer exists. It was that part of Old Melbourne currently beloved by the National Trust and the rich trendy—two-storey brick with iron-railed fence and cast-iron balcony, a tiny front garden in which weeds flourished until even geraniums fought a losing battle, and an equally tiny back yard, just large enough for stringing a clothesline. These terrace houses in the 'working class suburbs' (speech was less mealy-mouthed then) were dark, uninviting and subject to damp and cracking floors. By the mid-twenties they were decaying into history, and what they preserved of the past was better contemplated in photographs. With due respect to preservationists, redecorators and the National Trust, most of these places were dismal, insanitary rat pits.

Here reigned Grandma Gill, a tall, thin, impossibly angular harridan of fabulous age—fabulous because even her daughters could not discover the truth of it. Just before she died, in 1937, she claimed to be seventy-three; but she also claimed to have been in the chorus of the first Australian production of Wallace's *Maritana*, and for that she must have been over ninety. We doubted the *Maritana* claim, which had the earmarks of romantic accretion, but were disposed to believe 'over ninety'.

The importance of the *Maritana* reference (she would murder 'Scenes That Are Brightest' in a croak veering marvellously between contralto and screech) lay in its being my first intimation of our theatrical background. Grandma had been a chorus girl and so, it grudgingly appeared, had two of her daughters, my mother and my Aunt Linda. (This was romance in my widening eyes!) I discovered eventually that this suppression of facts was deliberate, enforced for what was in the social usage of the time a sufficient reason, and that Grandma's uninhibited recollections could set her circumspect daughters quaking. Only when her husband was dead, as were Grandma and my mother by then, did Linda one day show me the fifty-year-old clippings of reviews of her own performances and set the record in some sort of order.

Grandma—'Tot Lewis' on stage—was not the first of our family greenroomers. It seems, with typical obscurity, that there were two and possibly three generations of high-kickers before her. The tradition ended when Ethel and Linda married into respectability.

Grandma's repertoire of songs-around-the-house was limited but venerable. It included excerpts from *The*

23

Bohemian Girl and *Floradora*, as well as incoherent lyrics from something called *Tamba M'jaw*, which I later identified as Offenbach's *La Fille du Tambour-Major*, produced in Melbourne in the nineties. She had also played small parts (there are no stars or even minor leads in the genealogy) and could quote, with a most extraordinary accent, from a play she recalled as *Con the Shocker On*. Oldtimers may recognize *Conn, the Shaughraun* and place the accent as stage Irish.

She apprenticed both girls (there is no record of the other children in the theatre) to the stage with no more than the barely necessary education. My mother seems to have done nothing of note, but she was credited with a fine mezzo voice in a day when singing was prized as a social accomplishment. Linda was the stage baby who looked like being an explosion of talent and she collected good notices in Adelaide and Melbourne for a solo song-and-dance act. Eventually she landed a small character role in a Melbourne production of *The Belle of New York*, that of the drunken woman who gyrates through the choral finale of the first act, and seems to have filled it with sufficient abandon to 'stop the show'—which actually means no more than a personal round of applause. So much is true, confirmed by sources outside the family, but the follow-up (Grandma's version) is that a furious leading lady demanded that Linda be sacked for upstaging her. This is almost certainly not true; the tail sections of our family legends are usually detachable. We just can't help embroidering; I've caught myself at it often enough.

Linda, then, was the star *in posse*, the daughter with her foot on the ladder of fame. She put an end to those dreams by marrying, leaving the stage and behaving as though she had never been connected with it. Her husband was Malcolm Shepherd, a public servant already marked for promotion, who later became secretary to at least one Prime Minister, and finally, Defence Secretary. Such positions carried greater social cachet than they do now; class and context mattered, so Linda's past was dropped quietly into the dustbin of time. (Except by Grandma, whose raucous indiscretions kept everybody's boats rocking.)

I often wondered how they met, but never nerved

24

myself to ask. I can't imagine the stocky, serious-minded, unbending Sheppey playing stage-door Johnny with a bunch of roses—but it would be so humanizing if that were the way of it, even though between them they afterwards abolished all word of the licentious boards.

Linda was under-educated but nobody's fool. She learned the things that mattered—when to speak and when not, how to snub and how to set at ease, how to be a hostess or a guest or a dignified consort, and how to run the household of a man whose social contacts were an integral part of his professional performance. She learned mental poise, graciousness and reserve (perhaps something of gaiety was sacrificed), and reached the height of her experience in a display for which the theatre had given useful training—the approach, curtsey and withdrawal after presentation at the court of King George V.

My mother never forgave her younger sister that success. Her small-town triumphs were soured by the photograph of Linda in court gown and curving white plumes—all this unknown to me until as a young man I began at last to understand the silences, sullen angers and sudden spites.

Their careers ran parallel but not equally. Each married from the stage, beyond her expectations in money and comfort; each married a man more intellectual than herself, who lifted her into an unfamiliar style of life; each filled a position of respect in the society available to her. But Linda flew a higher orbit in a brighter system.

My mother could not bear to be outclassed. After her death I found her diaries and destroyed them, but whole passages remain in my junkshop of a writer's mind. A single sentence will do for all, an outcry from the time of our miserable flight to Melbourne, an expression of the rancour confining itself to secret words: 'but my children have charm and hers is . . .' Leave out the spiteful word. The bitterness overrated Frank and myself and libelled Linda's daughter, who indeed possessed virtues denied Ethel's disastrous sons.

These discoveries, made piecemeal over the years, had no meaning for the small boy fascinated by fabulous Grandma and immune to realities.

To her daughters Grandma was an old devil, incarnating in her scheming bag of bones the whole of the family urge towards drama, exhibitionism and romance. No amount of money was large enough to prevent her being broke on the day after receiving it; to raise more she frequented money-lenders, sold the furniture and gambled on horses. She posed to the neighbourhood as a broken-down old woman deserted by her spendthrift children (most of whom contributed weekly to her upkeep) in the hope of shaming them into giving more, and was not above threatening to offer her memoirs to the gutter press in order to cause productive embarrassment. In my young and secret heart I wished she would. I enjoyed her performances in the same half-hysterical spirit as I enjoyed film and play; she was my assurance that the world of magical outrage was not confined to screen and footlights. While the spirit of young Tot Lewis lived unchecked in Grandma, that other Lewis's Alice could flourish in my mind. The world's monotonies had only to be lived through until the wild realities burst out.

I still have a photograph of Grandma, sepia-tinted and stiff, taken in late middle age, theatrically poised and piercing-eyed, very *grande dame*—and not essentially different from the sharp-boned, toothless, cracked-voiced, three-quarters-blind old woman who played extortioner to her children and whistled up SP bookmakers in back lanes.

She claimed to be Spanish in one line of her descent, justifying prodigality and caprice as Mediterranean temperament, but her deeply darker-than-olive skin she passed off with casual mention of a Samoan gentleman two or three generations back—far enough back to gloss miscegenation as romance. Indeed there was a dark gentleman, but he was no Samoan: inspection of Grandma's broad nose, and the splayed nostrils of at least three of her children, tells with certainty that he was an Australian Aboriginal. In those days one did not admit to a touch of Aboriginal blood; there was nothing South-Seas-romantic about *that*. I wonder what his name was, and what his tribal emblems. I like the feeling of having some real connection with my country.

There's an off-beat, irresponsibly comic novel in Grandma but, alas, no room for it here.

In 1922 parents did not explain the private family shames

to their children, following the common wisdom that they could not be expected to understand and should in any case be shielded from unpleasantness. Perhaps they had some argument on their side; today, when children are shielded from precious little, and are in consequence faced too early with situations beyond their competence, we worry about the rising rate of teenage suicides. At any rate there was no explanation when our short flat-life ended and I was boarded out to strangers. If I was puzzled or unhappy or merely acquiescent, I don't remember; I don't even remember the strangers.

I know now that my father had made it clear that no further money would be sent (probably he had none; he had become a clerk in a hospital) and that my mother must fend for herself. And for me. Frank had cut pretty nearly free of us; he neither needed nor wanted a family.

No two of us ever again lived under the same roof.

It is necessary to take stock of my mother if the subsequent years are to make any sense.

I make no excuses for myself (and acknowledge no need for any) but she was unquestionably a *good* woman in that she lived by a puritanical code and never to my knowledge transgressed it. She resented the world that did not do the same. Scrupulously honest in all transactions, she disdained both lie and liar, and—I can express this in no better way— observed a contemptuous disapproval of sex. That her moral stances tended to a blustering righteousness was not an idea she could understand. Challenged, she would answer 'But I am right,' unable to conceive otherwise. I heard her say it, often.

I am sure that she never wittingly committed a wrong action; she *knew* the right, and did it. How she rationalized when events showed her wrong I cannot imagine, but I never heard her admit error or seem aware of one; fault lay in others. Her certainties extended to advising others of their errors before they were committed; in consequence she was respected, even admired for her iron virtues, and avoided. To the end I know of no-one who called her friend.

She wore her loneliness with anger, asking nothing of anyone, beleaguered in aggressive pride.

It was her pride that took so fierce a beating when at a stroke she lost home, husband and sustenance and, sold up and socially humbled, discovered in Melbourne that the son of whom she had hoped so much was a stranger. What made life at all possible for her was her sole cardinal virtue, courage. It must have provided its own dark satisfactions.

She could have moved into the empty rooms in Carlton, where Grandma rattled round two all but untenanted floors; she could have asked and received help from members of the family and so bought time to consider and plan. She did not, would not; she was capable of giving, not of asking. So she placed me in board with strangers, vacated the flat and took a position as a housekeeper. The rest of her life was spent in service.

In her view of fair deserts the fall could not have been greater or more unjust. Then Frank went to New Guinea to work and returned to Australia only once in the fourteen years before he died in Port Moresby in 1937. She was left with nothing but responsibility for a six-year-old son—an inturned, selfish and unloving child who took all and gave nothing.

That first boarding arrangement lasted only a few weeks before disagreement arose over a too-consistent diet of bread and jam and I was moved elsewhere. All I retain of the place is the memory of a book. Lord knows who owned it or where it came from, but it was called *Philippa in Upside Down Land* and was one of the host of *Alice* imitations that flooded the market after Carroll's huge success. The recollection confirms at least that I was reading fluently by the age of six. Other books are forgotten; only the fantasy remains.

In the same way fantastic Grandma remains strongly lit where other relatives are background figures, out of focus. Her madly elocuted declamations from dead melodramas, her tales of the never-never land of the theatre, and her callous riding roughshod over convention and good form, represented the exciting real world I lived only to one day enter for myself.

It is unnerving that the fantasies persist while all the rest blurs out.

The next three years are vague except for the

excitement of books. A new home was found for me with two ancient, practically extinct, English ladies—the phrase 'shabby genteel' could have been invented for them—with whom I lived for the next decade. They were background; what mattered was books.

Here Aunt Lucy entered my life, and unknowingly provided a further impulse towards a future of fantasy. She was my father's sister, living in Melbourne, and the only member of his family I ever met. She had me to lunch each Saturday and there can be no doubt that she was kind to me over a period of years—and equally no doubt that my interest in her was the weekly sixpence she gave me as tram fare home and entry to a silent-film matinee.

Saturday afternoon pictures for threepence! Heaven in a darkened hall! It is no accident that the films I remember best from those years of glory are *The Thief of Bagdad*, *Metropolis*, *The Phantom of the Opera*, *The Ten Commandments*, *Ben Hur* and *The Lost World*. Dozens of more realistic productions have left no stir or whisper.

Aunt Lucy—or rather, her husband, another Frank—had a large, locked, glass-fronted bookcase before which I prowled with longing until on my ninth birthday (only an ageing Edwardian aunt would know how she arrived at that figure of decision) I was permitted to open it and get my hands on the loot.

Most of it was school prizes two generations old—morocco-bound editions of Scott, Tennyson, Moore, in microscopic print—and Uncle Frank's legal reference works, but there were also a round dozen of novels by Jules Verne, and several of H. G. Wells's scientific romances. *From the Earth to the Moon, Twenty Thousand Leagues under the Sea* and *Journey to the Centre of the Earth* went down in giant gulps. The term 'science fiction' was years latent in the womb of time but in those Saturdays an addict-in-waiting was created. The words, the pictures, the fabulous adventures!

H. G. Wells was harder to swallow (but a child's greed is like a shark's—everything goes down), though he left the more persistent mark. *The War of the Worlds* was digestible, *When the Sleeper Wakes* less so, and the meanings of neither became plain until long after. Nor did *The Time Machine* have significance, though the cold and

29

menacing vision at the story's end, of an ancient planet under a dying sun, has never left me. Nor has any science fiction writer since provided an image to dethrone it.

Wells brought me no fresh vision of the universe; what his novels did to me was more subtle and in the long run more useful: they stirred the latent sense of meaning behind meaning that fixes the vision in rather than out.

Turning to *The War in the Air*, I got myself thoroughly confused between its fictional war and the Great War of 1914-18; unaware of publication dates and prophecies, I seemed to be reading about the same war coming to a different ending. I knew, as did any boy who read the juvenile weeklies of the day—*Chums*, *Pals* and the like— that the Great War had been a tremendous adventure, with our side on top, so Wells's insistence on ugliness and devastation troubled me. I mulled over Tom Smallways's last despairing words amid the wreckage of his world— 'it didn't ought ever to 'ave begun'—and wondered at last about *losing* a war. The adventurous jingoism was under-cut; misery was held up as one face of triumph. The idea was not clear to me, merely troublesome, a cloud between my mind and my pleasure.

I could not know that a circle had been closed. From a child's introverted 'reality' I had climbed into the fantastication of *Alice*, made a simple crossing to the more attainable dreams of Verne and Wells, and been drawn by Wells back to an understanding, however nebulous, that behind adventures lived people who suffered the perils without the high exaltations.

I could not know, either, that with Wells I had come to science fiction in its first brilliance, and that as a genre it was already in decay, that by 1926 it had fallen to a rock bottom of semi-literate childishness—and that its only possible direction, if it was to continue at all, was up. So the new science fiction and I grew up together, not always side by side, but never far apart.

Since we shared the way for the next fifty-and-odd years it will be as well to provide the genre with a back-ground and a genealogy. Science fiction did not spring fully armed from the heads of Verne and Wells; it had already a long and almost snobbishly aristocratic family tree, which is, happily, more accessible than my own.

3b
Where It Came From, What It Became

This essay in literary genealogy touches only on essentials and is not intended to be definitive. Its main aim is the elimination of confusing elements too often identified with science fiction.

If a genre is to be recognized as such it must feature some basic replication of structure (the classic detective story), subject matter (the historical romance), setting and characters (the Western) or other identifying convention. But what identifies science fiction?

It is a commonplace that no satisfactory definition of the term exists. Even Peter Nicholls, editor of *The Encyclopedia of Science Fiction*,* is on record as admitting that definition is not a likely possibility; the *Encyclopedia* notes a selection of suggested definitions but settles for none of them.

Critics and writers alike dodge the difficulty of fixing on a single attribute common to all the loosely related sub-genres and associational works sheltering under the name. While each reader and writer may have some personal definition, publishers and critics force the term on such diverse areas as 'heroic fantasy' (swordsmen, sex and sadism), science-fantasy (a bastard breed mixing science and magic), 'super-hero' comic strips (Flash Gordon, Garth, etc.), certain operas (*Aniara, The Makropoulos Case* and others—the *Ring* cycle and *Tales of Hoffman* are so far unclaimed)

---

* *The Encyclopedia of Science Fiction*, published by Granada (in the USA by Doubleday) in 1979, is a vast compilation indispensable to the student of the genre, containing many theme essays of great individual interest. This work may be updated from time to time but is unlikely to be superseded for many years.

and almost any cinema film showing a hint of imaginative licence. Editors and publishers use the SF label to promote grass-root sales of mindless trash, while writers and critics tamely accept the insult, too apathetic to launch a protest for honesty. All connive at the denigration they complain of.

An odd result is that what a few decades ago we called science fiction—stories having some basis, however shaky, in actual science—is today branded 'hardcore SF' and mistrusted by a majority of buyers. Science fiction that rests its case on solid fact and solid thinking is suspected of being fit only for eggheads and the mandarin literati, who in turn suspect it of being fit only for the intellectually unwashed.

To understand this unsatisfactory situation it will be necessary to discover how science fiction came into being. Here again confusion reigns.

Once, at a small Melbourne science fiction convention, when the question of definition surfaced briefly I suggested that Genesis must be included in the genre canon on the ground that it presents a consistent if doubtful cosmology. Nobody laughed; they thought I was serious. I haven't attempted deadpan satire with fans again.

The search for origins cannot range too far back in time to please the aficionados who seek to legitimize a genre that languished for years in the literary gutters. They pant after respectability. Ancient writings are hung on the family tree without sense or understanding; *The Epic of Gilgamesh* becomes an ancestral form because it features the Flood, a natural disaster and therefore scientific, Revelation because it is prophetic and therefore futuristic literature, Lucian's *True History* because it retails, tongue in cheek, a visit to the Moon, Homer's *Odyssey* as a prototype of the Vernian wonderful voyage, Shakespeare's *The Tempest* for reasons that elude me (Prospero's mirror?), Plato's *Republic* as the grandfather of all Utopias (which, strictly speaking, it is not), Plato again for the Atlantis legend in *Timaeus* and *Critias*, and finally *Beowulf*, presumably holding up Grendel and his mother as archetypal BEMs.*

Enthusiastic amateur historians see these and hundreds of other works as precursors of science fiction because they present specific preoccupations that figure in modern genre tales, but this is not enough to support a case; these books, particularly the oldest, are the ancestors of *all* modern fiction, and there is not much argument in claiming everybody's father as being specifically your own. Nor is it enough to characterize a genre in terms of special preoccupations. The sciences, particularly psychology and the other 'soft' disciplines, are a familiar element of all fiction, and are often treated more intelligently by 'mainstream' writers, in works that deal with the factual and social aspects of scientific and philosophic change, than science fiction has shown itself capable of doing. For the science fiction fan, however, rational thought is not enough: fantastication is required, a peering at reality as it is not and probably could not be. So the identity of his addiction becomes further blurred by emotional demands.

Is fantastication, then, the identifying element of science fiction? Hardly so, when the same elements are present in the same conventionalized form in the detective story, the Gothic thriller, the spy story and all the other production-line manufactures. Distortion of reality does not make an identification, but perhaps there is a *manner* of distortion that provides a clue. It may be productive to isolate the *kind* of unreality that attracts certain readers above other kinds.

To achieve this we can do something rarely possible in such a project: we can discover what the phrase 'science fiction' meant when it was coined, because we know when it entered the language.

In America in April 1926 Hugo Gernsback became begetter

* BEM = Bug-Eyed Monster = almost any large non-humanoid alien organism. Early science fiction writers were partial to giant insects (in America, bugs) as models for monsters, and illustrators favoured the huge, inscrutable, menacing insect eyes.

33

and editor of the world's first magazine devoted solely to what he termed 'scientifiction'. The clumsy word was soon domesticated to the more manageable 'science fiction' but its meaning remained the same; it was some years before interpretation broadened to the point where actual pirating of other genres began.

In Gernsback's view (and who could question the originating authority?) scientifiction was fiction about technological development, aimed at the type of reader who supported *Science and Invention*, his technical magazine, which also published some adventure-story scientifiction. The motto on the cover of *Amazing Stories* was 'Fiction today—cold fact tomorrow', affirming his belief in the *predictive* function of what he printed. This ideal decayed at once for shortage of suitable material, but at least he had seen a possible use (as well as a market) for a fairly didactic fiction with a suggestion of subliminal education (a worthy idea whose skids were soon kicked from under it), and given it a name.

He did not invent science-based fiction, merely created a focus of attention for it, and in naming it he only codified what had existed in essence for at least four centuries. A fiction of alternative life-styles, based on current knowledge and suggestive of possible developments—an intellectual ideal, whatever the shortfall in performance— was already established, though without an agreed name, in the public market. We must look at some of this material in the light of the Gernsback vision, which enjoined a number of imperatives:

(1) The use of fiction based on scientific fact or accredited theory.

(2) The use of fiction to examine the present world and suggest improvements or alternative modes of doing or living.

(3) The use of deduction and extrapolation to keep such suggestions within bounds of reasonable possibility or future possibility as the state of science itself improved.

(4) The insistence that change could be directed by scientific effort and not left to uncoordinated chance.

Gernsback was not the first to have the vision but he became its major apostle.

The literary ancestry of this ideal conception begins, as far as I can trace, in 1516, when Thomas More inaugurated the use of fiction as a tool for spreading philosophical ideas in an entertaining form. His *Utopia* is not scienti-fiction as Gernsback intended his invented category, but the form of it is; the content is sociological, and sociology was only peripheral to the Gernsback vision of a perfected technology ushering in an earthly paradise. He should be living at this hour!

The first book of *Utopia* deals with the social conditions of early sixteenth-century England; the second contains an account, by one of its inhabitants, of the land of Utopia (situated in America, God help us), where matters are better ordered. There is argument as to how much of the work is satire and how much genuine suggestion for improvement, but what matters here is More's perception of fiction as an ideal medium for dissemination of the idea that the world need not be the unsatisfactory place it is, and that the mechanisms for change are in our hands if we have the will to study and use them. *Utopia* is the first *deliberate* use of the method one day to be called 'science fiction'.

One hundred and ten years later, in 1626, appeared what seems the first true candidate for the Gernsback canon, Francis Bacon's *New Atlantis*. Bacon, a major scientist and philosopher of his time, added to More's social outlook the visionary notions of future science and of a state guided by scientists. Those who like to feel that science fiction can exert some positive influence may take heart from Britain's august Royal Society, which recog-nized Bacon as a major precursor of that organization through his description, in *New Atlantis*, of Solomon's House of scientific wisdom.

Other volumes by European authors followed. Few are remembered, and those are rarely read. Kepler's *Somnium* is an oft-cited forerunner but is more daydream than speculation; still, his intention was the awakening of interest by means of fiction. The wearisome 'Baron Munchausen' tales are claimed for science fiction by eager-beaver literary historians, although they were only fancies for jaded appetites and their use of 'science' was farcical. An enormous output of 'wonderful journey' tales, mostly by European writers, is mercifully forgotten.

Genre historians rope in Jonathan Swift's *Gulliver's Travels* to boost claims of classical lineage, despite the description of Laputa, on which the claim is based, being a violent and excremental ridiculing of science and the Royal Society. The four-pronged Gulliver denunciation of the human race has much to do with paranoid misanthropy, but nothing at all to do with the optimistic interests that created science fiction.

Mary Shelley's *Frankenstein* is also claimed, though its proper classification is the Gothic horror story, popularized by Walpole, 'Monk' Lewis and others. Her glossed-over handling of the 'scientific' aspects of the making of the Baron's monster indicates that this was not a major concern; what she wrote was a novel about a man usurping the creative privilege of God (the alternative title is *The New Prometheus*) and about the cruelty of humanity towards the alien. Her scientist is a miserable human eventually destroyed by his unholy creation; the creation, the 'monster', is a forlorn creature seeking love, becoming a figure of terror only when rejected with violence.

These aspects of her novel have been ignored in essay and film; only the horror survives. The horror certainly was intentional (she and the other dwellers in the Villa Diodati had agreed that each should write a horror story) but she manipulated an already established genre to enable it to make philosophic statements. Brian Aldiss, in his *Billion Year Spree*, makes a case for *Frankenstein* as the true progenitor of modern science fiction, but I feel that he has taken a side issue for the main achievement, in that Mary Shelley's invoking of science was only a useful step in the creation of the creature of pity and terror that was her literary aim. That she built much more upon it is to the credit of her intelligence and sympathy, but science fiction has remembered only the shambling figure of Boris Karloff murdering his way through a series of bad films.*

That Mary Shelley used a few trappings common to science fiction does not categorize the work. Theodore Sturgeon pointed out long ago that the introduction of a spaceship into a story did not create instant science fiction; neither, he might have added, does the introduction of any other 'scientific' gimmick whose only function is to maintain the excitement. As for Mrs Shelley's 'science', her description of the biological processes required for the construction of her unfortunate monster is limited to a single sentence: 'I assembled my materials.'

Frankenstein bequeathed to science fiction only a progressively cheapening taste for blood and sadism. Mary Shelley's spirit must be disgusted.

The scene shifts to America and Edgar Allan Poe, another 'founding father'. It is true that Poe wrote tales that can be classed as science fiction (less within the Gernsback definition than in the expanded meaning that has evolved from it) but his main influence on genre writers has been as a purveyor of outré horror. He seems to be a progenitor adopted with more enthusiasm than reason, and with total disregard of his real literary importance; his influence on modern science fiction has been minimal because he was an unusual talent—baroque, entertaining but immiscible in any genre pool.

Now, back to France, and at last the popular breakthrough, when Jules Verne brought to the newly literate classes news of the marvellous world lying just outside the borders

* *Billion Year Spree* (Weidenfeld and Nicolson, 1973) is a joyous but idiosyncratic outline account of science fiction. Aldiss sees the Gothic element as central to the development of the genre; this view, untenable in my opinion, though others accept it, leads to some distortion of the overall description of the scene. Lord Byron and his personal physician, Polidori, lived in the Villa Diodati in Switzerland in 1816, while Percy and Mary Shelley lived near by. All agreed to write horror stories, of which Mary's alone was completed. The scraps by Byron and Polidori surface occasionally in out-of-the-way anthologies.

of their education. If there must be a 'father of science fiction' he should be Verne, who not only wrote techno-logical novels aimed at anticipating the future but put such fiction once and for all on the readership map. His works were the definitive examples of what Gernsback had in mind.

The new literacy created a hunger for knowledge, which degenerated into a popular fascination with wonders, not surprisingly in the drab, industrial, nineteenth-century West. Verne's paragraphs, loaded with statistics and explanatory passages reading like textbook extracts, are tedious today, but they were part of the wonder then, and still part of it in 1926, when Gernsback's fledgeling contri-butors used the same techniques. (All those minute descriptions of super-gadgets, backyard spaceships, and future cities like New York ten times higher!)

Verne opened science fiction to every level of readership by delivering his wonders in the form of adventure stories. Speculation was no longer the province of the schoolmen and the educated rich.

The next major work in the genre appeared in America in 1888—Edward Bellamy's *Looking Backward: 2000-1887*. This, beginning as simple fantabulation looking thematically to More's *Utopia*, developed, in its author's words, into 'a vehicle of a definite scheme of industrial re-organization'. He postulated a more or less socialized state, but for story used the device of a contemporary hero waking after a century in hypnotic sleep. This allowed the new world to be assessed from simultaneously present and future points of view. Writers are still devising new ways of achieving this, now that time travel and anabiotic freezing have become clichés.

As prediction, *Looking Backward* fared as poorly as most of its kind; conceptions of the ordered state have changed out of Bellamy's strait-laced recognition. (So has the direction of science fiction; the modern writer disavows the predictive function, and indeed the genre's record in this area is lamentable.) Still, his focusing on social as well as technological development continued the direct line from More and Bacon.

It was left to H. G. Wells in England to inject a warmer humanity into the mode in a series of novels wherein the protagonists were everyday folk confronting the incomprehensible; he placed his emphasis on the impact on their lives of new conditions not necessarily equated with progress. He was the first writer of consequence to ask 'What will be the *human* effects of these inevitable changes?' and with the question he established the real value of science fiction as a vehicle of commentary reaching through generalized conception to the individual man and woman. His science fiction is still read, is still relevant, and sets a literary standard equalled by few of his genre successors.

His humanitarian approach established the distinctively English school of science fiction writing wherein change is the impulse rather than the end. Many such novels were written in England after Wells turned his attention to other themes, but most were of transient interest until the 1930s. A brilliant exception was J. D. Beresford's *The Hampdenshire Wonder* (1911), probably the first fiction to grapple in psychological as well as emotional terms with the theme of super-intelligence, and more recent assaults measure poorly against it.

In America the situation deteriorated. Nothing of enduring quality appeared for decades after Bellamy. The gap was in some degree plugged rather than filled by the 'Tom Swift' juvenile novels of technological invention, and by hectic romances such as the Martian novels of Edgar Rice Burroughs. The Burroughs brand of delight scooped the pool of magazine readership with cloak-and-dagger plots transferred to rich alien surroundings. Other writers, such as Ray Cummings and Homer Eon Flint, extended the range of venues to cover the atomic microcosm and the fourth dimension (presented as a real place) but did little to disguise the essential melodrama of their product.

In *Amazing Stories* Gernsback reprinted Verne and Wells while he waited for new writers to appear, but when they did so it seemed that those who followed the editor's idea of 'scientifiction' were abominably bad writers, while those with any fictional talent preferred the high jinks of Burroughs and Cummings. Since the majority of readers came down on the side of high jinks, within a couple of years the new fiction had collapsed into self-imitative silliness. Yet in this era of awfulness it gained a hold on Depression America, and on Depression England too, possibly because an inexpensive escapism was a psychological necessity of the time. More magazines were founded and standards sank lower yet as small talents were spread transparently thin.

With improvement or extinction the only options for the genre, it was a good time for the future critic and novelist to enter on his involvement. He was eleven years old and avid for fancy in a grey existence.

4a
Directions

From ages six to nine everything not centred on myself is nebulous; even my mother fades into the background. As a housekeeper she had only a half-day free each week; domestic service was callous and demanding. In that half-day she had to find time for her personal needs, visit Grandma Gill and visit me in my boarding house. So I saw her for only a couple of hours each week.

There were days when she managed to take me to the theatre, which was considered an essential part of my education. The commercial theatre was at a low ebb, and in any case the family taste had never risen above the hack material its members had appeared in, so the cultural gain was negligible. We saw, from two-shilling seats in the gods, harmless shows like *The Five O'Clock Girl*, Tivoli vaudeville or a revival of *Charley's Aunt*, but my real interest was in the Aladdin's cave of the silent screen. Saturday afternoon with Lon Chaney or Douglas Fairbanks surpassed the pale pretences of the stage.

I have the impression of an unaffectionate, secretive mouse of a boy who loved only solitary pleasures. Books and the Saturday films were the retreats from a world greyed by the remoteness of grown-ups who did not give explanations to a child and refused to credit the existence of a child's observing mind. Alone in an adult society, my reaction was to shut them out whenever possible.

Self-sufficiency began; I remember unhappiness but never loneliness. Those who call childhood the happiest days of their lives have only my doubting credulity; I wouldn't wish a replay on anyone.

The maiden ladies with immediate control over my life were relics of a social order effectively dead by 1922.

Miss MacIntosh was small and squat, strangely mannish I thought, possibly because of her large nose and dark shadow of moustache. She was the forceful one of the pair, the decision-maker and bearer of burdens. She was English and tiresomely conscious of it, but her memories of Britain seemed confined to a famous train wreck (in the 1880s at Leighton Buzzard in Bedfordshire), how the Flying Scotsman thundered through stations creating a gale that whirled luggage into the air and skirts over heads (she probably believed it by then) and the collapse of the Tay bridge. She had a taste for rail disasters.

She had some memory of how the English 'quality' spoke in that receding day and aped their speech in an affected dropping of the final g, as if to align herself with the huntin', shootin' and fishin' county society. It is still heard now and then among south bank Londoners. The short i was emphasized, giving a lilt that I strove to emulate, and was promptly stopped. That was mimicry. But if that was correct speech, why . . . ? Well, I mustn't, and that was that. The matter was filed in the you-wouldn't-understand category.

She insisted that I call her 'Auntie', which I supinely did without warming to her genuinely good intentions.

Still, I preferred her to 'Nahnee' (heaven knows where that name originated), whom I identified at once as enemy. Miss Leyland was cold, fragile, faintly transparent, a wearer of ill-health as a halo above petticoats enough for a polar winter, and a filler of conversational gaps with oblique references to her refusal ever to complain. I thought her a professional malingerer, which may have been unfair, but my childish eye noted her as capable of doing anything she wished but tending to fainting spells (old-fashioned hand to brow while groping for support) when unattractive activities loomed.

She probably did suffer minor ailments and with them

42

created an impression that constitutional delicacy was inseparable from the business of being a gentlewoman, finely nurtured and of real if unemphasized distinction. She was stiff with gentility and a final authority on grammar, protocol and manners. She was deferred to not only by Auntie, who seemed a willing slave, but by the boarders. Perhaps they laughed behind masks of polite deference; I merely disliked her.

These ageing women would seem to have had little in common, but after half a century much is plain that a child could not understand. That they were good-hearted and well-intentioned, and that they loved each other with the desperate dependence of those whom a changing world had passed by, is apparent to the backward gaze, though one was pretentiously common and the other a spinster in the discard. They had the resigned courage of those who expect nothing, and enough spare loving to bring up a ward, Bessie, whose relationship I never knew and probably never questioned. The girl was nearly adult and none too happy with constant reminding of how much she owed her selfless guardians. Selfless they were, but they were also relics of a Victorianism that demanded that the dependent be aware of her state and properly grateful, and show it.

The time came when something of this demand was transferred to me and the weight of it killed any sense of gratitude in me for ever. It was apparent to me—at an abominably early age for such pragmatism—that people do what they wish to do, or wish to be seen to do, or are constrained to do, and that even a gift of love is a pleasure to the giver. Gratitude is a sense of being beholden, and I will not be beholden to another's pleasure.

A friend gives and I accept because giving and sharing are acts of friendship, acknowledgements of a state contenting both parties; if I give and the recipient is at once in a flurry over the non-existent debt I become impatient and inclined to withdraw from contact. The debit and credit system of balancing human relationships seems to me one of the great barriers to genuine respect and affection. To foist it on children is monstrous. You can't buy or command a child's love; you can only give your own and

43

not complain if you don't obtain an equal return. Complaint is the fast road to rejection.

In the first three years with them I fancy myself only in the role of lurking brat, solitary with a book.

Where the books came from I don't know, but in that house I got through great loads of R. M. Ballantyne and G. A. Henty and volumes of myths and fairy tales. Later, from Aunt Lucy's store, I obtained along with Verne and Wells the novels of Sir Walter Scott—and read straight through the twenty-five volumes of the Complete Novels. Today I find only his Scottish tales bearable, and not all of those; what a book-greedy child will swallow whole is incredible. Omnivoracity, if I be permitted the word, describes it.

After three years the maiden ladies sold up their boarding house. Nahnee's 'turns' made the housework, of which Bessie did the lion's share, too much for her. They rented a shop with living quarters in rear, in Elsternwick, and stocked it with second-hand items for sale and second-hand books for exchange. Bessie, having no relative, went with them, and my mother arranged that I did also. She was no doubt at her wit's end, and they glad of the board money.

This was 1925, when incomes were frighteningly low by modern standards and money values difficult to compare with today's. In the houses of the poor—and we were the poor—the rise of a halfpenny in the price of a two-pound bag of sugar or a one-pound block of butter was cause for calculation and careful shifts. I was aware of poverty from the mealtime litanies of providence but it did not touch me. I was never hungry beyond the normal greed of a child; if I wore poor clothes I was unconscious of them; I had my Saturday afternoons at the pictures and the occasional penny for sweets, and I had books to read. Being unaware of other things to want, poverty had no meaning and the tragedies of others no existence. Books were my world. I was allowed such books from the exchange counter as Nahnee declared suitable, but I read without her permission, too; by age ten my range was well up with that of an educated late adolescent.

There came a change that at last roused some perception of a world outside my introverted head.

Since the household had moved about four miles, it became necessary to find a new school for me, and Nahnee made a suggestion with immense impact on my future. True to her erratic gentility, she suggested a school of what must have seemed to her semi-magical provenance—the Choir School of St Paul's Cathedral, Melbourne.

My mother's intolerance of religion must have been negated by desperation and Nahnee's seductive depiction of a 'public school' education and training without fee. My mother had, I discovered, respect for Nahnee's gentility and social erudition. Accomplished poseurs themselves, the Gills were suckerbait for the conceits of others.

Nahnee's impression of education at St Paul's was most likely based on hearsay of the son of a friend's friend, a one-time St Paul's boy praised as a gentlemanly young fellow. It would have been enough for her innocent snobbery. The report of education in manners and speech turned out correct, if skin deep; all else was peculiar.

I was given a note and sent alone (since the maiden ladies could not cope with the terrors of the City) to attend an audition for prospective choristers. By some small miracle I penetrated the warren of offices and meeting rooms behind the cathedral and found the Chapter House.

On a small stage, seated at an upright piano, was a thin, bald and beaknosed man who seemed to be the focus of attention of the assembled boys and guardian adults. With the instinct of the loner I chose a chair sufficiently isolated to deny identification with the whispering many. That reflexive recoil from absorption in a group has never left me.

I caught the bright blue eyes of the beaknosed man assessing my solitude.

Names were called. Boys mounted the stage to be engaged there in short, soft colloquy; a chord or two was

45

struck and the unfortunate (most of them miserably uncomfortable) sang and returned to his seat. When names ran out, the very blue gaze pinned me. 'Who are you? What is your name?'

His voice is still with me; I had never heard English so clearly and beautifully spoken. I was petrified, aware but bereft of sense.

'Is that a note? Why don't you bring it to me?'

It must have been sweating in my hand for an hour or more. I climbed and stumbled with it to the piano. The note was read and the beautiful voice asked 'And what are you going to sing for me, young Turner?'

The next dialogue is lost in the confusion that must have engulfed both of us until at last he struck a note and said 'There! Sing your song without a name.'

I sang in shaking unhappiness, and when at last I ran down like a tired squeaker doll he said 'That song is called "Brahms's Lullaby"'—said it very quietly as if in some conspiratorial compliment. Then he wrote on the bottom of my note and sent me home clutching my acceptance for the choir.

Where, in God's name, had I learned the Brahms 'Lullaby'?

Doctor Alfred Floyd, Organist and Choirmaster, an English musician of talent who had chosen to make his home in Australia, was an extraordinary personality, one of those 'unforgettable characters' of whom you later realize you have learned nothing deep or revealing. He was birdlike, short and spare, thrusting his head in a quest for worms of wisdom, leaning his body after with hands behind, so that in talking he pecked at words while cocking a bright, expectant eye.

He was temperamental, enraged by incompetence, often blindingly and sometimes brilliantly insulting, and most understanding of the young and lost. He refused to treat us new boys as learners fumbling a study of musical elements while around us younger but more experienced lads moved easily among the mysteries. When things became difficult he gave a brief lesson to the entire choir, never singling out our ignorance. He knew what many a teacher never learns, that a child will accept a dressing down with the proper display of submission (tears if required—there is always a modicum of role-playing) but will not soon forgive humiliation before others. The only recognition of our novice state was that we did not sing in a cathedral service until he was satisfied with our progress.

How he monitored progress puzzled me greatly; that he could detect the tone of each individual voice among two dozen was inconceivable. There had to be a knack to it. 'Knack' was a word in much use for explaining away the inexplicable abilities of others—such as a discriminating ear.

His system worked—for everybody but me. At the end of four years I had not mastered the groupings of acci-dentals called key signatures, and could read music about as well as demotic Greek. Thirty years later, in a chance meeting, I confessed to him that I had dissembled ignorance to the end, and to my acute discomfort he took excessive blame for it, as though some carelessness of his had doomed me to life in a condition of musical insensibility.

I loved the music—lots of Mozart, Handel, Bach, Brahms, Purcell, Mendelssohn—and was able to memorize anthems, psalms, magnificats and the rest in a single rehearsal, even to exactness of initial attack at the proper point in the introduction. That I got away with it is hard to credit, but so it happened. This opacity to musical elements has left my appreciation almost wholly sensual; intellectual and technical content I glimpse rather than grasp. So, after soaking in the music of the eighteenth and nineteenth cen-turies it took me many years to grope towards Ravel, Stravinsky, Janacek, Britten. Composers like Bartok and Ives remain purveyors of alien sound, but the huge reper-toire accessible to me is more than I will assimilate in what's left of a lifetime.

My voice was no more than FAQ but I was filled with the joy of singing, however mediocre the noise. There was almost unendurable joy in the whispering mystery of 'God So Loved the World', the rocking near-waltz of 'For He Shall Feed His Flock', the exultant yell of Stainer's operettaish 'Fling Wide the Gates' or, during Nativity recitals, the down-dropping melody of a dozen boys representing angel voices high up in the lantern gallery. It was a joy that had nothing to do with religion and everything to do with psychological release. It was the same tension that strained and choked in peaks of enthralment in books or the spectacles of the screen—with this difference, that as singer I was *creating* the joy.

If I could recover anything at all of those years I might choose the return of that ability to respond totally in unspeakable rapture and wonderment. It recedes with time, thinned by repetition and familiarity, dulled by intellection, flattened by critical dissection.

Eight services a week brought me no closer to God. I doubt that I ever consciously listened to a sermon (*Magnet* and *Gem* were then the choirboy's undercover reading matter; what curiosa they hide under their cassocks today boggles the imagination). The other boys were similarly unengaged. Any amusement would do to pass the time of the service, from the spreading grin of the overweight tenor in the cantoris stalls at the Psalm verse 'All ye who are fat upon Earth have eaten and multiplied' to the occasion of young Heriot's breaking the rowdiest fart that ever racketed through that hall of echoes and reduced our two dozen charmless souls to aching, silent hysteria.

Charmless indeed. As a group we existed in a state of internecine feud, taking instant sides on any matter or, when open warfare palled, gathering in a righteous group about some unfortunate convicted of social error, to shred him with the cruelty of birds at a wounded fellow. Heaven help (but it never did) the victim betrayed by incautious word or deed! The only semblance of fair play rested in the certainty of each one sooner or later enduring his turn in the psychological stocks.

Over this loutishness lay the screen of our voices: if we learned little else, we learned to speak well. Doctor Floyd insisted on fine diction; we were given dramatic words to sing and the words should be heard. So when he corrected our pronunciation it was his Wykehamist accent that we absorbed, and very Wykehamist it was; it took me thirty years to lose the accent I learned from him.

Doctor Floyd may have communicated tone to speech and

intangibles to the spirit but the educational branch of the Choir School seemed to be a species of poor relation.

The choir schedule required an hour's practice each morning, Monday to Friday, evensong at five o'clock each weekday afternoon, additional services at Christmas and Easter, a round of carol-singing visits at the end of the year and the occasional choral wedding. Schooling was fitted into the cracks.

Choir practice ran from nine till ten, and the school was a mile and a half distant in East Melbourne, so lessons began at eleven and ended at four. With an hour for lunch, that meant four hours a day for secular education. An intelligent boy could be taught most of what matters in that time, given good teaching and small classes, but our curriculum and conditions were marvellously impractical. The school itself was a church hall, unsuitable for the purpose and reached by an ancient, cobbled back lane; it may still be there, piously mouldering. We two dozen cherubic young louts were divided for teaching purposes into approximately equal groups, under-12 and 12-and-over— all in the one room.

This arrangement fell apart as bright young scholars were shunted too early into the senior group, where they were regarded by their peers as upstart swots, while the not so bright were held back for an additional year, which laid them open to peer treatment as congenital idiots and subjection to pitiless shames at playtime.

Who designed the curriculum must have had delusions of classical grandeur. Coming at the age of nine from the comparative simplicities of a State School, I found myself up to the choking neck in Algebra (and I still fresh from chanting, 'five fives are twenty-five, six fives are . . .') as well as Latin and French, both matter for tears in early weeks. Other time was filled with History (Alfred and the cakes standard), Geography ('the principal exports of Brazil are . . .'), Arithmetic, English, Grammar, spelling bees and even Religious Instruction. I suppose that little active harm was done, but when four years later I moved to a school less intellectually exotic I found myself three years ahead of my age group in French, saddled with a Latin no longer taught, mathematically inept, and utterly at sea in everything else except English Composition.

Despite the large elements of hit or miss in our instruction much of it must have clung. Later, when I began seriously to write, I valued the grounding in extra languages, the early recognition that the wonder of words lies as much in their kinship and ancestry as in meaning and flexibility.

The school had no playground and no allocation for sporting gear. We took our lunch break in the nearby Jolimont Park and for recreation depended on invented games. Even cricket and football were invented games because we had no materials with which to play them in any but the sketchiest fashion. So we welcomed amusements requiring only the simplest instinctive organization. These, as previously noted, could be unpretty.

The peculiar circumstances of the Choir School created an unlovely kind of schoolboy. It has to be assumed that we all grew out of our special savagery when our voices broke and we returned to civilization. Perhaps, perhaps not. (The Choir School no longer exists as such. Soon after I left, the boys were sent to Trinity Grammar for secular education, and would have mixed there with a less tribal sort of youngster.)

As one with no gift for friendship, I drifted through the Choir School years without making any permanent mark or suffering any permanent scar, not altogether solitary but forming no attachments. My attitude was one of waiting; this was a thing happening to me that in time would come to an end . . . Music made the waiting bearable; that and the sense of language were the loot I carried away at last—but real life, as ever, began at any moment when I could retire into my fantasizing self.

There was something schizophrenic in my existence, as though part of me was the extroverted hoodlum of the choir and part the withdrawn lump of all other occasions. The secrets of my 'real' life were shared with nobody; a hint of deviation from the norm observed by my fellow brats would have laid me open to vivisection in the lunch breaks. What piddling privacies each one of us must have guarded against the scorn of his peers!

Yet the secrecy of my internal life was broken, by my

own fault and in an idiot fashion that both exposed and saved me, and science fiction was the cause.

Hugo Gernsback's *Amazing Stories* appeared in America in 1926 but did not reach Australia until the following year, intercontinental transport being then slow to yawning point, but in 1927 I saw its first gaudy cover hanging on the wire rack of the old McGill kiosk at the foot of the Post Office steps—and I was lost. Verne and Wells and Rider Haggard rose up in recognition, and that magazine I must have.

The price was one-and-ninepence, a large sum to an eleven-year-old and expensive by the standards of the day, but I had been engaged in petty theft for some time and found the means to 'decorate myself' (P. C. Wren's Foreign Legion novels were part of my current reading) with the money. I was detected, but more of that later. For the moment 'scientifiction' had arrived and I was riding a winged steed.

In the same year I found the Martian romances of Edgar Rice Burroughs and discovered my vocation. I would be a novelist, a romancer of far worlds, strange beasts and mighty machines. I would write 'scientifiction'. I began my first novel almost at once. It was called *The Prince of Mars*, but it owed nothing to Burroughs's *A Princess of Mars* other than setting, characters, fauna, flora and plot. It filled a notebook, perhaps twenty pages of round script bulging with monsters, rayguns, swordfights and princesses rescued from immurement in the dead sea bottoms/dark canals/ramparted cities of Mars.

Why I should have had this secret volume with me one day at the cathedral is beyond my present imagining, but in the usual feral scuffling to enter the lift that took us up to the practice room I dropped the notebook. With the inevitability of fate it fell open and flat and was picked up by that jackdaw of curiosity, Alfred Floyd.

'Writing, eh, young Turner? Essay?' Why should he have imagined an essay? It might have been a diary, and private, but his swift eye detected fiction. 'A story! May I read it?'

Painful, whispered permission burned lips that dared not refuse—one did not *refuse* an adult—and knew by the surrounding silence that a nonconformist victim had been delivered over to grubby cruelty. And all that day it was so.

Yet final triumph was mine when after school we returned for evensong, and marvellous old Flop, who could shame with a word and transfix with a glance, returned my novel with a pat on the head and his conspiratorial grin, and in front of the assembled choir told me that I had a marvellous imagination and must develop my talent.

Surprisingly, this stopped all persecution; Flop's praise was sparing and respected. What he saw in my plagiarized scratchings is beyond conjecture, but it is at least clear that his reading did not include the Martian romances of Edgar Rice Burroughs.

Let the small boy rest for a few pages. Prying at his egocentric mind is not easy; a rest will benefit him and myself. Staring inwards hurts more than just the eyes.

4b

In the Direction of
the Rubbish Heap

More than one contemporary science fiction writer has
called Hugo Gernsback the worst thing that ever happened
to the genre. His short pre-eminence was no gift to style or
intellect, but those so quick to despise him might be without a market for their wares if he had not existed. Most of
them are too young to have read the material in the
context of its time, of which they have only secondhand
opinions; others, old enough, are merely graceless.

Gernsback had a didactic conception of his field,
exemplified by his barely readable novels, *Ralph 124C 41+*
and *The Ultimate World*. In fact his personal range was
narrow and his extrapolation timid, but anything in the
way of a heat-ray, spaceship or television device was
wonder enough in 1926. Though it was claimed that he
insisted on scientific plausibility in the stories he published
(his own plodding products were models in this respect),
as an editor whose magazine had to make financial ends
meet he knew better than to insist on anything of the sort.
His writers did not, for the most part could not, attempt
scientific sense; those who tried confined themselves to
textbook lectures and lists of planetary statistics compiled
from works of popular astronomy.

In early issues of *Amazing Stories* he published many
novels and stories by Verne, who fitted his standards
exactly, and Wells, who did not. He published little else
with any pretence at factual backing. Consider such novels,
very popular with the readers, as *The Moon Pool,*
A Columbus of Space and *The Blind Spot*, and ask 'Where
is the science?' The answer will be: 'Not here.'

53

Brian Aldiss, though observing that 'this dictat was more honoured in the breach than the observance' (one more misunderstanding of that much abused line from *Hamlet*), debited it with having 'the effect of introducing a deadening literalism into the fiction'. While admitting his ground for irritation, I feel that he missed the point. What there was of literalism proceeded from the ineptitude of Gernsback's recruited new writers (some in their teens, we are told) who often allied promising ideas with a total lack of talent for fiction—and all too often, little talent for English grammar. Gernsback's was a preparatory role and his 'dictat' provided only the testing ground for the re-direction of science fiction achieved later by John W. Campbell. There were always a few writers who respected factual rather than 'invented' science and who gradually attained some literary competence; it was they rather than the romancers who made modern science fiction possible. The deadening literalism was less the effect of intruded science than of lifeless inspiration and writing.

The stories were in retrospect awful, but they were read, and the monthly letter column of *Amazing Stories* carried argument over scientific plausibility as well as juvenile put-downs of authors guilty of misrepresenting the surface gravity of Ganymede or the radius of the orbit of Mercury. The interest was serious if naïve. In spite of their awfulness we read these tales and asked for more—but who were *we*?

Surveys run by the magazines of the late 1920s and early 1930s (via rather loaded questionnaires) suggested that many of us were engineers, doctors and minor scientists, tertiary students and teenagers. Accent on youth. A whip-round of authors suggests that these same groups supplied the writers. MDs and PhDs were flourished in many a byline (Keller, Breuer, Lemkin, Smith *et al.*) and many a first sale seems to have been made by a student. Jack Williamson certainly wrote his first published story at 19 (fifty-four years later he is writing science fiction still) and John W. Campbell was a student when his 'When the Atoms Failed' opened his extraordinary career.

The signs suggest that *Amazing Stories* was a young,

crude venture appealing to a young, crude public, the only sort of public whose naïve hunger for marvels could persist through years of juvenility until a more literate and intellectually responsible product emerged. It was to remain a 'product', packaged corn, for a long time, but it is unfair to lay all the mush at Gernsback's feet. He did what he could with what he had, and his real service was to centralize the *idea* of science fiction by creating a specific market. He provided, almost single-handed, the milieu for the critics and writers who denigrate him now.

A glance through a few issues of *Amazing Stories*, 1926-28 vintage, must cause wonder at our lack of sophistication as well as the voracity that could make such rubbish pay. Science fiction had established its first popular following—on the critical rubbish heap.

I had joined the following as a juvenile criminal, and if we did not thereafter go hand in hand through life, we rarely lost sight of each other for long.

5a

Growing Lad

During the Choir School years I became more aware of my mother, and not for the betterment of our relations.

Her life ran from grief to grief. In her first housekeeping position her room was broken into and stripped of what little she had kept of clothes and jewellery. I found the account in her diary, bare but crying out—'all my little trinkets'—and for the first time was pierced by the pain of a spirit I had thought (if I had thought at all) impermeable. She never allowed people to see past her set face. Neither, it now occurs to me, did I let any see past mine.

For twenty years she worked as a servant in the homes of others. It was a savage time for domestics; they had no union and no redress for injustice; in a time of despairing unemployment they had no recourse but to bear with what they could get in the way of a roof over their heads, three meals a day and minimum pay. Hours were long, late into the night if the mistress entertained, up to seventy hours a week with little hope of an extra pound for extra work. *Lucky to have a job* was the understanding on both sides of the bargain. The pay in 1929 was twenty-five or thirty shillings a week and keep in the better homes; God knows how little it was in the homes of the middle class who kept up the vanishing 'style' of a help in the house. Wages were reduced as the Depression ground on; the poor took what they could get.

My mother's pay (she seemed able to command a better than average wage) would have supported a single woman, who could have dressed and even saved on it in the economy of that time. But in the murderous climate of dole and hunger, who was not supporting someone else? How she managed to board me and clothe both of us is past my guessing, when she had to contribute also to the upkeep of Grandma Gill. She did it and even maintained a small and fiercely guarded bank account.

The pain of service, of being at the beck of people with whom her sister Linda was on visiting terms, must have been exquisite—though Linda had a keen sense of the hurt of others and would never enter a house where her sister was employed.

What hope my mother may have placed in her sons was barren. The elder deserted for the security of a job in New Guinea; the younger, secretive and unresponsive, showed suddenly as a sneak thief.

The occasion was that one-and-ninepence for *Amazing Stories*. On a visit to Linda's house I saw the needed couple of shillings on her kitchen dresser and took it. The loss was not noticed until the milkman looked for it next morning; by then I had my magazine.

Nobody saw me. Therefore nobody could say I took it. How unfair, then, that Linda should at once suspect me and keep on insisting 'But you did take it, didn't you?' until resistance ran out at my guilty fingers' ends. What followed, when she told my mother, was the first of a series of floggings that dwarfed all punishments of the past. It put me to bed for two days, too bruised to walk and shocked by a ferocity of rage that had been more terrifying than the pain.

Discovery of the theft struck deep into my mother's puritanism; what struck deeper was the fact of the theft having taken place in Linda's home, demeaning her pride in her children. I paid for the looting of her heart, the stealing of one more dream from a dwindling store.

In the ensuing three years the performance was repeated half a dozen times, not always so severely. That the beatings did not deter my thieving fingers remains a mystery, with every foray made in a terror of discovery that was actually a certainty of discovery. The stealing seems to have been compulsive. Defiant?

When it stopped it stopped suddenly. I don't know why, but the perception that my mother had no control over her rages may have had something to do with it. What had seemed a simple cruelty, a determination to injure, I recognized as a simpler thing still, an inability to stop until an internal agony was released. She had no-one else on whom to discharge disappointment and loneliness. Any prim suggestion that she should have exercised self-control would be the cant of an ignorant virtue knowing only small temptations; she sought purging and peace from her anger at pride forced into subjection twenty-four hours a day at the demand of strangers.

It is easy to look back in understanding and without anger, to make concession to human fallibility, but to the teenage boy it was brutality, irrespective of cause and effect. It was a war that twisted the minds of the combatants, and one that ended as swiftly as it had begun, without official truce, leaving behind a waste of resentment that neither of us was ever able to cross. We achieved a sort of sullen armistice. And that is all that need be written about it.

Music-making with the choir came to an end midway through 1929. I was 'expelled'—a word that in the mouths of my maiden ladies took on an awfulness of disgrace I did not feel. In the more casual language of the choir, I was sacked.

I was in fact sacked twice. The first time was in company with two other boys, the reason one of those unfunny practical jokes (concerning rotten fish in the lift-well) that convulses the perpetrator and infuriates everyone else. The Precentor, responsible for choir administration, was assuredly furious. Our dismissal came from Doctor Floyd, who folded his hands behind him, leaned forward like King Stork rejecting undersized frogs, and said 'Goodbye. Go home.'

I heard, later and unofficially, that while agreeing with the necessity for sacking he had been highly amused. This and his sympathy with the child mind may have had something to do with all three of us being reinstated after a week or two in the wilderness, but our return provided him with opportunity for one of those bursts of fiendish insult that occasionally overcame him.

With the three of us standing in show of penitence, he made a few remarks larded with apt biblical quotation about prodigal sons—and concluded unexpectedly with that altogether unamusing text 'As a dog returneth to his vomit' (Proverbs 26:11, if you care).

The other two never forgave that remark, but I, familiar with the fine language of the King James version and vainglorious with literary expertise, had to cap him with the rest of the verse: 'so a fool returneth to his folly'. I think it surprised him, but he said only 'You may be right.'

A month or so later I was summoned to the organ loft in the middle of evensong. He glanced sideways at me as he played. 'Go away. I'm sick of you. You talk too much.'

I can only assume that my voice had been raised in chatter above the permitted whisper. The return to folly had been brief.

The maiden ladies displayed genteel shock but my mother's reaction was muted; she may by then have decided that disappointment was her life's norm. And so it was.

The years between expulsion from the choir and finally leaving school are strangely disconnected in recollection; incidents obtrude in no particular order, as though much has been consigned to some amnesic dustbin. Only the beginnings of literary obsession are clear.

From the choir I went to a State School, where my 'English' accent was praised by teachers and derided by my fellows, and where I had to adapt to a whole new order of peer behaviour—less constricted, less vicious and at first misunderstood.

As an outcome of the insane curriculum of the Choir School, my Latin and French were useless to me. My spelling and essay writing were more than adequate and my spoken and written grammar pretty near faultless (more than can be said of them today) but of parsing, analysis and the rules of syntax and composition I was paradisally ignorant; I had to learn, with fury and a sense of desecration of sacred places, the shoddy structure of rules guiding the literary faculties I exercised as naturally as breathing.

There was a shock concerning the nature of Science. The Choir School had ignored the subject, but by 1929 I had absorbed two years of *Amazing Stories* and had my own idea of what Science was about. My understanding encompassed a grotesque collection of prehistoric animals, spaceships, super-weapons, cities run by atomic power, drugs creating minds of genius, the fourth dimension, and Atlantis awaiting discovery on the seabed. In the magical realm of Astronomy, meaning space travel, I had off pat the orbital dimensions of the Solar System, the masses and surface gravities of the planets and major satellites, together with much information (all now known to be incorrect) about their atmospheres and temperatures, and a slew of conflicting theories about the ice-caps of Mars, the cloud cover of Venus and the origin of the asteroids.

Quite a few scientists, mainly in America, have claimed that science fiction fired their youthful imagination and led to research. I'm willing to believe them, but my first acquaintance with real science bid fair to cure me of the subject for ever. Winds and tides, the formation of clouds and hail, why lightning strikes, the working of the thermometer . . .

I set it to one side, denying it any connection with the Romance of Science. As it happened, my interest in science fiction was waning, though not to the point of relinquishment, possibly because fresh realities assaulted daily but mostly because I experienced a literary revelation of an unprecedented kind.

Finding Rafael Sabatini's *Scaramouche* in the local library I read the opening sentence—'He was born with the gift of laughter and a sense that the world was mad'—and fell once and for ever in love with the power of literature to create a universe, not in a complex of mighty deeds and shimmering descriptions, but in a handful of simple words, and with the blinding revelation that the world is people

61

and attitudes and ideas, not manipulated *things*. Every word I had ever written was disowned in that moment.

In an essay, 'The Lost Childhood', Graham Greene has written of the power of even a bad book to evoke response in the child mind; his crucial encounter was with Marjorie Bowen's almost forgotten *The Viper of Milan*, another historical romance. Mine happened to be *Scaramouche*, which is in no sense a bad book, only a harmless one—and that opening sentence performed the trick of evocation and perception. It is only a thumping, unrhymed couplet pretending to be prose, but crude tools can jemmy open doors; all the magic of words and meanings was there.

At fourteen all revelations are definitive. I needed only to deny the past and begin afresh. Old manuscripts, never completed, with opening sentences like 'The space ship captain's powerful body sprang into action as the meteor crashed through the vision port and precious air screamed out through the deadly hole' were laid aside. New daydreams began.

The new dedication brought upheaval from an unconsidered direction.

In my State School we were discovering Shakespeare, after a fashion, and some of my reserve vanished in exhibitionism as a reader in class. My rendition of 'Is this a dagger which I see before me', beginning in low-voiced fear and rising in controlled crescendo (courtesy of choir training), can have had little to do with the meaning of the speech but was an encore success for the class and a few none-too-literate teachers.

By what I suspect was juvenile boasting on my part, word of these performances reached my mother and she laid plans. Old theatre acquaintances could be revived, Linda could insert social tendrils at a managerial level, I could be given suitable speeches to prepare and an audition arranged . . . That the talking screen had closed all but a few of Australia's 'legitimate' theatres and that these eked bare subsistence from proven revivals played by proven public favourites was ignored. Some apparent professional interest (probably friendly but specious) was aroused before anyone thought to inform me.

I at once shattered one more of my mother's dreams My memory of what took place is imprecise, but it seems that I flew into the single really blazing tantrum of my whole life, announcing that I would be a writer and nothing but a writer, that I loathed the stage (untrue), and for once in a way convinced all concerned that the project should be dropped.

What is very clear is that my mother, when the dust had settled, suggested that since I was to be a writer it would be as well for me to display my writings. This was treacherous ground; I had in fact written nothing since the lightning-strike of *Scaramouche*, had been satisfied to dream of shelves of books bearing my name. While I wriggled and procrastinated a triumphant Nahnee produced for examination an exercise book containing a story beginning 'The space ship captain's powerful body . . .'.

I had not known that my hiding places had been found by adults with no conception of privacy for a child. Sacred files of *Amazing Stories*, now joined by *Wonder Stories* and others, flaunted their appalling covers whereon carnivorous flowers dragged explorers to their dooms, spaceships sliced at each other with red and golden rays, monsters slavered after fleeing nymphs, gigantic machines ground cities into rubble, goggle-eyed aliens . . . I recall Nahnee crying 'They're turning his brain! I can see it turning!' A statement I accepted literally, in dumb fright.

My mother's more lethal logic linked these lunatic pleasures with lacklustre school reports. So this was how I wasted my time! There would have been little profit in protesting that I had by now progressed to Sabatini and P. C. Wren; every child knows that whatever time he wastes on his pleasures should have been wasted on something else.

The storm broke in a memorable hiding. I must have bellowed the place down because the old ladies rushed into the street to assure passers-by that they were not responsible for the murder within. It puzzles me to recall that in later years my mother and I laughed together over the spectacle they must have presented in their trembling assurance to strangers that they were not child-beaters.

There must have been oddly human moments in that sullen mother-son relationship, if only in shared contempt of others.

This climax passed and I settled down to write—stories, poems, plays and innumerable first chapters of novels planned on a gargantuan scale, all fallen to dust and just as well. At least determination had crystallized, and now some sort of domestic peace set in.

Peace fled when in 1933 I failed to pass the required six subjects for what was then called the Intermediate Certificate. I failed Science, that loveless discipline that had destroyed the romance of space, time and the fourth dimension, replacing delight with the triangle of forces, problems in heat transfer and chemical formulae, which to this day I cannot manipulate with confidence.

It was doubly humiliating, not only because I did well in the other subjects but because at seventeen I was a year older than others in my class; I had never recovered the ground lost at the Choir School. Still, my last school, University High, gave me, besides two excellent English teachers, two years of the German language, which led to *Das Nibelungenlied* and via Valhalla to the Icelandic sagas, the Irish and Welsh legends, early English history, Malory, Chaucer, Marlowe and back to Shakespeare with newly opened eyes. A marvellous cycle of exploration. I was learning something of what 'literature' meant and becoming uneasy in contemplation of it. Unaccustomed humility had a foot in the door.

These advantages came slowly into what I still thought of as the real part of my life; immediately, the failure in Science meant that schooling was over and I must go to work. (I passed that exam easily a couple of years later in order to qualify for the RAAF, but the Air Force found no need of me. By 1939 I was glad to have stayed on the ground.)

These were the worst years of the Depression but nepotism found me a job. Keith Murdoch, father of the present newspaper magnate, was managing director of The Herald and Weekly Times and a friend of Linda's husband,

Sheppey. With Sheppey's backing I bypassed the usual department heads—personnel departments as we know them did not then exist—and was interviewed by Murdoch.

He, uninterested but conscientiously doing his favour for Sheppey, chatted about matters that seemed irrelevant, then demanded abruptly 'What do you read?'

It was a paralysing question to a mind whose preferred reading had ranged from the Bible to *Tanglewood Tales*, to James Oliver Curwood and Algernon Blackwood, *The Moonstone*, *All Quiet on the Western Front* and *The Skylark of Space*. It was like that impossible 'Have you been a good boy?' 'Everything,' I said, because no other word seemed practicable—and then, with conscious dilettante snobbery, 'Not stuff like Edgar Wallace, of course.'

It was a lie and it got immediate come-uppance. 'You should,' Murdoch said, 'he's an excellent journalist.'

So he too kicked my literary education along, opening up the immense subject of taste and its proper application, as well as teaching me something about ignorance.

I did not become an instant journalist; I never became any kind of journalist. Murdoch, duty done, despatched me like every other junior to the Messenger Room, where buzzers buzzed and clacking numbers told which department needed a pair of feet, and we boys ran, neither knowing nor caring about the meaning of the errands we carried out at lunatic speed. Eventually I was allocated to the Commercial (accounting) Department, where I totted up endless figures of daily newsprint consumption.

I was adrift in an adult world, without a peer group whose ways I understood, surrounded by men and women whose concern extended no further than my ability to fit in with their disinterested work group. I did not fit in. Friendless, with a mentality enclosed by books, living a home life directed by old women as little in touch with the world as myself, I must have been naïve beyond pity and socially helpless. I dealt with circumstances in the only way I knew: work became an extension of the school situation, a place where I did what I must until the day ended and I could return to reading and writing.

Like something peeping from a hole I observed the adult world without understanding. My immediate boss was a luckless gambler whose time and money went into the making of complex betting deals round every floor and department of the building. He was persistent as only a driven loser can be; each week I had the job of delivering, confidentially, an envelope to his loan shark. Most of the others seemed to be either drunks or too ulcerated to risk drink. I saw much and comprehended nothing, having no experience with which to compare.

I made no friends and did my uninteresting work with a matching lack of interest. The drunks and dyspeptics, for all their absences and time-wasting, got their work done; I, secure in my contempt of them, never succeeded in doing mine satisfactorily, and after three years of errors and omissions I was sacked.

I was not quite twenty-one.

I had coasted through the Depression with no thought of myself as part of a human gestalt; I was a unit, competently serviced, rarely making a decision because decisions were made for me and I had only sullenly to adapt.

Novelties in my situation now were that I had moved to a boarding house where I paid my own board, and that I selected and paid for my own clothes. In everything else I was constantly reminded that I had no legal right to my own decisions until my twenty-first birthday, 8th October 1937. That reminder was fast running out of time when I landed in the job market, up for sale with no saleable talent. I had never been required to do anything useful; I didn't so much as know how to look for a job and, having found out how, discovered no openings for a latent novelist too old and too inexperienced to be worth a living wage.

It would be idiotic to say that hard experience made me grow up fast, but my system did receive shocks enough to kick the instinct of self-preservation awake. A problem of board sharpened the situation. My mother offered no help, nor did I ask for it. Shame? Some stir of independence? I don't know. I think she waited, with some interest, to see what would happen.

What happened was that I drifted into becoming a casual waiter, one who instead of holding a regular job worked on wedding receptions, dinners and social functions. Casuals received a better hourly rate than permanent staff and I found that I could earn nearly as much working on three or four functions a week as in a full-time job; though table waiting was then considered a socially degrading occupation (and diners often treated waiters as dirt), I found it comfortable enough for my purpose.

A new and shopsoiled education commenced. There were few sleazier social groups than the casual waiters of a big city; they all knew each other, watched each other like weasels, guarded their 'good tip' territories with ferocity, dealt smartly with competition, stole what wasn't nailed down and drank any liquor left unguarded. Perhaps in forty-five years, with caste distinctions fading, this may have changed and casual waiting become a preserve of gentlemen. I doubt it.

The workplaces were mainly hotels; inevitably I learned to drink. That is, I took to occasional drunkenness almost from the acquisition of a taste, and soon stepped up 'occasional' to 'frequent'. By the time Hitler's war broke out I was well on my way to alcoholism. The word was not then in my lexicon and in any case represents a condition discovered in yourself only long after everybody else has diagnosed it. It was the beginning of a long haul and, despite the cautionary tales, not altogether an unpleasant one.

I note it here only as an activity whose consequences were far in the future, because the major effects of alcoholism do not make themselves immediately felt. The other compulsive habit, smoking, began at the same time and escalated as rapidly to fifty or sixty cigarettes a day, and the two indulgences managed many years later to come within slicing distance of killing me, but in the beginning they were simply pleasures and for a long time remained so.

That such compulsions were rooted in the psyche was not then commonly recognized (pop psychology had to wait for the cinema of the 1950s) but it would be easy in hindsight to pinpoint a solitary childhood as favouring these facile dampings of terrors and uncertainties. Aside from the unfairness of laying blame on people who did their best under unreasonable pressures, the eventual working out engages me more than the hypothetical causes, and will appear in its proper place.

During these years I wrote with greater concentration and dedication than ever since, pouring out hundreds of thousands of words, all in longhand, a Niagara of ink splashing paper. None of it was submitted for publication. With a perceptiveness hard to reconcile with so great a self-centredness I knew the stuff was no good. Some may have been publishable but it was not *good*. A cold-blooded critical faculty seemingly detached from the self saw that the characters creaked, the descriptive passages fell dead and the dialogue was affected chatter; the plots were close to plagiarism, the drama melodrama, the humour sophomoric.

With a sense of high calling embarrassing to look back on, I determined never to submit a manuscript for publication until it satisfied *me* that it was fit for others to see. It was a decision that deprived me of potentially useful editorial comment. For right or wrong I held to this idiot determination; twenty years and a war passed by before it and I were satisfied.

There's ruefulness in looking back on such a critical absolute. Then I *knew* that the stuff was insufferably below standard; nowadays the feeling is more a hope that it is not pocked with betraying crudities. There's ruefulness, too, in the reflection that never since those days of ecstatic rubbish-making has there been such joy in the act of creation. There have been later, deeper satisfactions, but never the pure joy.

5b
Growing Genre

It must be emphasized that my outline account of the classic origins and gutter breeding of today's science fiction is only an outline, excluding much. Its *raison d'être* (aside from the recounting of a perennially exasperating love affair) is to explain how the chaotic situation described in Chapter 3b came about. The faithful will decry my rejection of all influences before Sir Thomas More as nebulous or secondary, others my refusal to be impressed by *Frankenstein*; many will find my synoptic view at variance with their own—but there is as yet no 'official' line. So, to business:

Amazing Stories suffered bankruptcy and changes of ownership but the name survived (still survives) under other editors. Gernsback started other magazines but it soon became apparent that his approach was too narrow, his authors too plodding and their talents too small. By 1929 it was time for the professionals from the crime, Western and adventure magazines to move into this new market, and in 1930 they did. Prolific hacks like Arthur J. Burks, Charles Willard Diffin and others were assembled under the Clayton banner to feed romantic adventure to the new *Astounding Stories of Super-Science*. Out went the 'science', which was in most cases little loss; in came megalomaniacal invention and hair-raising adventure wherein villains snarled, heroines were captured and heroes toppled empires singlehanded. It was just what the reality-bound Great Depression needed—a limitless wishdream at an affordable price.

The injection of professionalism into an amateurish

venue was itself good, but a few thoughtful writers and editors began occasionally to publish stories that looked to a more sophisticated public; editors like Harry Bates and F. Orlin Tremaine were aware of a public for whom suitable adult material was not yet available in quantity.

In 1937 young John W. Campbell Jr, fresh out of college and already the author of a string of grindingly super-scientific space operas, became editor of *Astounding Stories* (its title cropped and simplified), and for more than three decades he remained the most influential figure on the genre scene. Strangely for a man whose writings had so far displayed an astonishing bluntness and insensitivity, he set about reorientating the genre to a humanitarian viewpoint as well as returning the 'science' to fiction in stories that would observe the effects of change on human existence.

His horizons, however, were limited, as his polemical, condescending editorials demonstrated, and his assessment of humanity was strictly behaviourist; his philosophy of science was that of an empirical engineer—if it works, it's good. He had also a mulish dash of imperialist racism. This unpromising combination, allied with a quick perception of what readers did *not* like, made him a compulsive and often persuasive preacher (on any idea that struck him as he mounted the pulpit) and fostered a whole generation of writers who preached along with him—for money. Together they peopled a universe wherein aliens came off second-best to ingenious Earthmen, engineers and physicists always routed businessmen and politicians in confrontation, extrasensory talents were the next evolutionary step forward, and a solidly imperialist USA was the only source of progress, freedom and common sense. Still, he brought a sense of science back into the field and some needed stylistic improvement.

By 1939 he had launched Robert Heinlein, Isaac Asimov, Theodore Sturgeon, A. E. Van Vogt and Henry Kuttner. All but one remain prominent today; by the wickedness of fortune the one who died, Henry Kuttner, was incomparably the best of them. Campbell's private interest in ESP, telepathy and 'wild talents' favoured stories with these as themes and was a founding factor in the unstemmable gush of rubbish that seems unable to function without at least one possessor of super-talents as a major character. (This enables the writers to resolve all situations without recourse to intelligent plotting or, indeed, intelligence.)

Campbell made one other innovation, which is not only too much with us but has contributed immeasurably to the present state of generic confusion. He started a companion magazine to *Astounding* and called it *Unknown*.

Unknown was an attractive escapist-fiction product whose stories operated on the zanier side of magic and occultism without too much emphasis on shock/horror, capitalizing on a logical rather than fantastical resolution of supernatural situations. The new idea aroused some entertaining fiction, but more primitive mice soon emerged from the woodwork. Fritz Leiber's 'Two Sought Adventure', first of a forty-year line of 'Grey Mouser' stories, introduced what came to be known as 'sword and sorcery' into an early issue, and it proved popular and only too easy to imitate. Since the readership of *Unknown* was very much the readership of *Astounding*, and since many of its stories straddled an indistinct borderline between science fiction and romantic fabulation, the difference became blurred in readers' minds and has been so ever since.

In-group critics, confronted with the hybrid, tried to justify what was there (to the extent in some cases of deciding that science fiction must be an offshoot of fantasy) rather than make the effort to sort it out. So-called 'heroic fantasy' (a more reputable-sounding name for 'sword and sorcery') of a formulaic kind became linked with science fiction in the public mind and played its part in preserving the conception 'cheap and stupid' of a genre that deserves better.

Like most innovators, Campbell left problems and debris behind him and it is fashionable now to decry him as sternly as Gernsback, to complain that he held science fiction in a straitjacket for twenty years and prevented freer conceptions arising. He did nothing of the sort; other avatars came when their time was ripe and without effort secured the changes of direction needed, while Campbell watched uncomprehendingly. The truth is that he found science fiction in the gutter and at least dragged it on to the footpath and dusted it down; later practitioners mounted his shoulders for their wider take-offs. He was a man of great energy and severe limitations who achieved a deal of good amid the muddled bad.

Britain was another matter. While American science fiction was struggling with literacy problems, across the Atlantic a different vision was making fugitive appearances.

Olaf Stapledon's panorama of evolving humanity, *Last and First Men*, was published in 1930 and attracted critical attention for its logical (from Stapledon's premisses) but controversial musing on future history. Its vast scope, following evolution for the next two million years, made it the most intellectually far-reaching and meticulously detailed work to appear in the history of the genre. And having written 'genre', I pause to reconsider.

Stapledon used all the apparatus of the science fiction of that day—evolutionary change, the rise and fall of empires, alien species, interplanetary warfare—but used it in a sophisticated fashion that had little in common with the simpleminded inventions of pulp fiction. Nor did it exhibit many of the elements of the conventional novel; its few individual characters were transient figures illuminating the attitudes of transient cultures, and there was no plot in the narrower sense of the word; it demanded intellectual attention without continuing characterization, dialogue or moments of domestic climax to carry the interest. It suffered, despite the magnificence of conception, from a vocabulary plain to the point of dryness. Yet it remains a masterpiece, solidly hewn and wonderfully inventive. Its fate was to be hailed by 'mainstream' critics and read by a discriminating public (in fact by the audience for which it was written) and almost ignored by the science fiction world. It made no impression on the genre writing of the time and nothing else like it emerged until Stapledon's own *Starmaker* (1937) formed a companion piece pondering the immensity of creation and the diversity of life forms throughout the universe. There is some doubt that Stapledon, whose interest was predominantly philosophic, had any idea that he was elevating a fallen genre to the stars it so ineptly coveted. In any case science fiction, offered the cosmos, settled for blood and guts.

Stapledon roused the interest of the intelligentsia and the opposition of such religious thinkers as C. S. Lewis but made no impact on an earthbound genre unprepared to absorb intellectual jolts or even acknowledge their existence.

In 1932 Aldous Huxley made a much bigger public splash with *Brave New World*, which, though radically different in tone and technique from the genre product of the day, can be seen now as traditional science fiction. It extrapolated from a present situation to a future development, paid respect to the facts of biology though using them satirically and created an outré though essentially believable future. Its warning against biological dictatorship caused great argument, and its cynical observation of repercussions on sexual behaviour, harmless enough in all conscience, were by many objected to as tasteless. Looking back, it can be seen as a direct descendant of the manner of Wells and Beresford—smooth, thoughtful, pointed and resistant to the temptations of melodrama.

Only a readership as insensitive as that of the pulp-devouring 1930s could have remained unaffected by the knowledge that the three best science fiction works of the period made their impact and their sales *outside* the genre ambience. At the same time, only a dilettante literary snobbery could have been in that same period unaware that these objects of its critical and intellectual interest were one with the 'lurid space stuff' with which no self-respecting litterateur could risk association. If it was good, it couldn't be science fiction.

Both ends of the writing and publishing spectrum failed to observe opportunity, and America continued to grind out the mixture as before at one cent a word or less.

One mildly intellectual British novel of the period found favour with genre readership—C. S. Lewis's *Out of the Silent Planet*. However, 1938 was too late for changes in direction; the next year would have smothered them under the necessities of war. The book was in some degree mystical, and its evocative language created an aura of strangeness exactly right for the fans of the 1930s, but it also coated the metaphysics with sufficient emotional chocolate to render them unobtrusive. Science fiction approved, but again it was the non-genre readership that appraised the book at its proper worth.

The four British novels noted here sold well and are still reprinted. There *was* a public for quality science fiction in the 1930s, but the cheapjack influence of the pulp magazines ensured that few writers of quality would risk the mode; they feared that their reputations might suffer under the science fiction cloud.

Meanwhile the writers and readers of *Astounding Stories* and a growing number of similar publications were complaining of being confined to a literary ghetto and of their field not receiving proper critical and intellectual attention. They were right about the ghetto but unable to see that they had built it for themselves with their shoddy work and their openly expressed resentment of the literary snobbery of the 'mainstream'. Campbell made it plain in a couple of his coat-trailing editorials that he had no time for the 'literary' approach; he wanted good yarns and, as controller of the highest paying market for the genre, he got what he wanted. As for 'proper critical attention', it would have killed most of them out of hand.

For all his peculiarities, Campbell was finally successful in constructing a better-furnished ghetto, but he was no Moses to lead his writers altogether out of it. That was left to others, but their banners with richer and stranger devices had to remain furled while a World War was fought.

6a
War as High Adventure

As a race we cannot be altogether unteachable, yet the experience of the Great War of 1914-18 taught nobody anything. Even the armies didn't make the simple observations consequent on new inventions and changing modes of thought, and twenty-one years later were caught with their horse-drawn limbers in the mud by a mad Austrian corporal.

In literature—still the most persuasive of the media—the cry from the heart of Remarque's *All Quiet on the Western Front* (a willing but inadequate attempt at the disgusting truth) was drowned out by such sentimental jingoism as Raymond's *Tell England* and the tough-gutted-but-tender-hearted, grin-and-bear-it war stories of 'Sapper' (H. C. McNeile). The British boys' weeklies retailed gung-ho adventure in the front line and at sea, making sure the kids looked forward to their own exciting baptism of fire. The American pulps did still better: they put out 'adult' magazines with titles like *Battle Aces* and *War Birds*, celebrating brawn and guts and helping Dad also to look forward to the next hero-time.

Sanity had no chance against romance. Here in Australia the Anzac story became increasingly the Anzac legend as facts receded in memory, and the misty veil of old mateships rendered the whole ghastly business proudly acceptable, even to the crippled and the bereaved.

A humanity blind to facts was ripe for a fresh bout of mass murder, and got it. And has been getting it in various parts of the globe ever since. As I write there are at least five highly publicized wars in progress around the globe, as well as others that have dropped out of the headlines and are of interest only to those struggling to survive them. The unengaged remainder wait with something like apathy for the USA-Russia confrontation of idiots to initiate world-wide destruction—possibly by accident, providing a bang, a whimper and a cosmic giggle.

To this day I do not know why I enlisted immediately the 1939 war was declared. Whatever it may have been, the impact of having to live on floor-level terms with mass humanity terrified my ignorance and isolationism. Hell, as Sartre noted, is others; cheek-by-jowl contact with the common man was a descent into the furnace. I had to realize that I knew nothing useful or realistic about my fellow men, not how to talk to them or understand their interests or credit them with intelligence or good will. I had mind enough and desperation enough to learn quickly, but only on rare occasions during the next six years did I feel at one with the company of men.

In psychic chaos it was not possible to observe rationally the process of being turned into a soldier. Four decades later I sorted it out in my mind for a key passage in a novel, *Yesterday's Men*, and this is how it seemed to me, staring cold-bloodedly back.

> [A man of the late twenty-first century is speaking with a military historian. The soldier, he is told, was not a brute, but an ordinary man:] '. . . an ordinary man who killed at the order of other ordinary men. It's hard to follow.'
>
> 'Like this: From the moment of enlistment, personal degradation began in simple separation from his womenfolk and the conventions of civilization. You'll never have seen a group of young males *forced* to live together, all strangers and all released from the restraints of women and family and friends. The skin peels back from their minds; cultural safety is dissolved; they're out of the burrow with no way back. The sense of territoriality, of the group, is destroyed; each must assert himself or go under—and both things happen. Braggart alliances assert

themselves in aggression and numbers; the weak take on passive protective colour. The male animal thrashes about in proof of his maleness, in noisy language and physical provocation and aimless quarrelling. Sexual repression exhibits brassy stridency or goes sullenly underground to break out in squalls of violence or stupidity. The observer says, *so that's what they're really like,* but it isn't so; it's what they are like under disorienting conditions. As simply as that, men in the mass are laid open to manipulation, and manipulation is what the Army supplies. It's called discipline— twenty-four hours a day discipline, remorseless and nakedly oppressive, with even the so-called off-duty time supervised and open to cancellation without warning or explanation. That's where the degradation grips. The Army takes away the tetherstones and sign-posts of normal life, turns a man into a creature of confusions and then imposes its own version of order upon him. Civilized man is born to order; disordered, he takes to discipline like a saint to salvation. He hates it but he clings to it, lost without it.

'In the name of holy discipline he becomes a machine. He lives on food fit for scavengers because he'll eat it or starve; he lives cold and sodden because he's taught it's no hardship to a proud soldier; he crawls on his guts in mud, takes pride in senseless ceremonial drills, jumps at the command of brainless nits, takes public cursing from foul-mouthed instruc- tors, works till he's ready to drop and then carries on working—why? Because from the moment the barrier drops between him and his culture he becomes less than a man and knows it and has no self-respect other than the thing he is told to be. That there may be killing at the end of the road, or being killed, is neither here nor there; obedience and discipline alone can carry him through to the blessed goal of discharge. That's the soldier, the final product of a deliberate process of degradation: a Pavlovian dog. He can be shocked out of it—he sometimes is when the killing starts—but in general he behaves as a faithful hound.

The joke—if there is a joke—is that the masters are as response-conditioned as the dogs. It's a vicious circle of command and react. Only a powerful mind can remain his own man in the Army.'

Corrigan pushed his mess tin away . . . 'A calculated process of debasement.'

'In the strictest sense, no. It evolved across millennia of warfare, refining itself with use and habit. The leaders meant well. They often called it, Making A Man Of Him.'*

In this existence-by-formula I could rely only on largely irrelevant talents to avoid being swallowed alive. This meant, in practice, seeking the company of like minds. For the sanity of all concerned, minds like mine were fortunately rare, and slowly I was forced to admit the existence of a largely good-hearted and intelligent community, with myself as odd beast out. Loneliness was no new experience; I got through the first weeks more smoothly than my coddled resentments deserved.

The resentments were furiously fired when men who had never heard of Mozart or Thomas More outclassed me in every activity. I learned to watch their behaviour and assume the required masks, which were generally less feral than those of the casual waiters.

One absurd advantage paid off without my planning it. I had the facile family memory for 'lines', and the stylized military instruction (brain-deadening but unmatchable in its single-minded efficiency) stayed with me almost word perfectly. I could fumble a rifle like a village idiot but I learned the theory behind drill and weaponry at high speed and found myself suddenly in charge of a section (honorary and stripeless), to my surprise and that of the section. The men, more worldly wise than I, accepted me as one more trick effect of the impenetrable military mind and gave no trouble; they were as uncertain as I where the limits of rebellion lay. After a while they discerned advantages in a section leader who tried his inept best to look after them, and even assisted me over my larger lapses. I found

* *Yesterday's Men* (London: Faber and Faber, 1983), pp. 78-9.

unexpected satisfaction in being responsible for the welfare of others, but no time to ponder over it.

When we were sorted into units I found myself in the 2nd/5th Australian Infantry Battalion. I don't know why it never occurred to me to transfer to some more interesting and safer branch of the Army while transfer was still relatively easy. I suppose I was too busy navigating the shallows to notice the nature of the river.

What my mother thought of my enlistment is hard to say. Her only comment was: 'The men of the family always had their brains in their boots.' Oracular but unhelpful.

War is only intermittently interesting—and then frenziedly so; it is, as some forgotten commentator put it, utter boredom broken by moments of intense fright. A few moments of fright are worth relaying to those whose ideas have been coloured by popular fiction.

After a year or so of training in Palestine and Egypt the attrition of transfers and sickness had left us short of officers, so our platoon sergeant, Rex Samson, acted as platoon commander and I, as senior corporal, took over the sergeant's duties. Rex was not long out of 'the Shop', as he called the University of Melbourne, and his head was full of music, poetry and art. We became friends in the unsentimental manner of people with interests in common but little common outlook. The platoon became restless at our intellectual approach to matters of ordinary common sense, and later I discovered that the men had not been too happy about being led into their first action by a couple of airy-fairy 'brains'.

We moved up to the start line outside Bardia and bedded down as best we could in moonless pitch dark. I was wakened before dawn by the most demoralizing crash of sound I have ever heard. It seemed to come from a point next to my eardrum and in fact almost did: in black night I had gone to sleep practically under the muzzles of a battery of twenty-five pounders, and what wakened me were the opening roars of the pre-dawn barrage. Nothing ever again frightened me as much as that unholy salute.

With first light the battalion advanced in strung-out lines across the flat stony desert that covers the whole coastal plateau of Libya, and the Italian guns answered ours. We, the troops, were their targets.

Walking into shellfire over open, coverless ground is a stomach-churning business. The noise is appalling, the whirr of saw-toothed shrapnel intimidating, the sense of targeted loneliness like no other loneliness in life. Yet it all passes. You don't become accustomed to shellfire—never that! You learn to put up with it, to treat it as background irritation.

Needing the comfort of talk, I left my proper station in the centre of the platoon and moved to the front with Rex, who was probably pleased since he did not order me back. A few shells banged around us, uncomfortably close, and we bolstered each other's nerves with loud jokes and wonders of persiflage. This seemingly insouciant behaviour of their two precious intellectuals made an uncalculated impression on the platoon, who were as scared as we but not to be outclassed by a couple of NCOs they didn't think much of. So much for the example of courage: the ersatz product works just as well.

There was nothing that day to be heroic about; we trudged and sweated across uninteresting terrain, under the fire of enemy guns, towards a point where our Engineers had opened a gap in the Italian perimeter wire. And when we reached it the Italian infantry were using our gap to march *out* to captivity, in a seemingly endless line, content to have done with the unrewarding business. We were happy enough to feel superior but had no faintest understanding of why they chose to surrender in thousands. When we had learned something more about soldiers as human beings we did understand, and thought much better of the Italians than did our folks at home, who swallowed whole the newspaper accounts of fascist faintheartedness.

Inside the wire we came under much more concentrated artillery fire; the Italian artillerymen were professional soldiers, not conscripts, and had no intention of walking out of the war. Nor did they; their batteries had to be reduced one by one and they died at their guns.

State of mind is difficult to interpret. This incident may illustrate what I cannot dissect:

About midday a ration truck trundled its way to us through the monstrous noise and desert heat. Provisioning is a platoon sergeant's responsibility, and I collected from the truck a kerosene tin containing bully beef and biscuits in the proportion of one tin and one packet to three men. The platoon had halted in a shallow depression, relatively safe from shrapnel, so I was able to call up the section leaders and hand out their rations, to discover under the tins and packets a layer of the small, wrinkled oranges of the Levant. There were forty-three. The number is imprinted on my mind for ever, with the question: How to distribute forty-three oranges among thirty-two men? You need some experience of corporals fighting over their sections' ration allocations to realize that this, to nerves stretched in an ambience of unending hundred-and-twenty-one-gun salutes, was no ordinary dilemma.

A close shellburst jerked me to realizing that while I brooded the platoon had moved on. I chased after them, carrying the wretched tin of oranges and deciding that I would give each section leader a couple of extra fruit and let *him* tackle the distribution problem. Feeling Machiavellian, this I did. Last to come for rations was Ned Rosier, a large good-tempered redhead, who dropped the things down the front of his sweat-rotten shirt and held out a huge freckled hand for more. As an orange passed from my fingers to his the air came alive to the whirr of a piece of shrapnel, spinning like a murderous little buzz-saw, and the orange fell neatly in halves between our hands. Ned giggled like a madman and made his joke of the day: 'Half your luck, mate!'

Later, sucking a dried-out orange while lying on my face as if that would hide me from the gunners, I told Rex of my catering problems; he protested with demented pedantry that I should have *explained* to the corporals why they had too many fruit, absolute fair play being essential.

81

Such were the real priorities of us actors in the great drama.

There were darker moments, but I have to strain after them: the Italian artillery observer shot to pieces in his twenty-foot tower, shot to so many pieces that his blood drenched the whole wooden scaffold, clear to the ground—or the lonely Italian infantryman with his foot blown off, unable to understand that we would not kill him out of hand—or the young Australian lieutenant, mad with the pain of a hand mangled to rubbish and threatening to shoot the desperate corporal trying to calm him. The horrors tend to hide under the ash of time.

A more cherishable memory is of a rawboned corporal, whose name I have forgotten, saying how much Rex and I had kept up the men's spirits with our ratbag chatter. I had the good sense not to tell him that the spirits were our own, not the men's. He was a fine NCO, and I modelled 'Corporal Kane' on him when, a decade later, I wrote *Young Man of Talent*.

The Italian defences were circular forts dug into the ground and protected by wire and tank traps. On the second day we stormed one of these with artillery firing on us over open sights from less than quarter of a mile away. 'Stormed' meant running like hell through the deadly accurate shelling and tumbling head first into the cover of the tank trap—which was full of Italians. They were only mildly interested in us and content to be overrun.

We discovered in minutes why they did not fight. Their officers, who were conspicuously absent, had treated them like cattle. They were quartered in the tank trap, and their living conditions, particularly as concerned hygiene, were indescribable; they lived literally in a latrine without seats or covers. We learned much about the desperate side of human nature in one stinking day there, and no longer needed to wonder why the Italian infantry lacked morale. A soldier is only as good as his leaders, and these were not led but driven. There was much individual courage amongst them but it was wholly individual, having nothing to do with duty.

Tobruk was a rerun of Bardia—endless walking over a

stony plain, with gunfire. My Company was in reserve; if anybody fired a shot it would have been by mistake. Here an awful dullness set in and lasted until we left Africa.

We sailed for Greece, and there suffered for Churchill's obsession with the Balkans and the Black Sea, just as our fathers had suffered for it as uselessly but far more bloodily at Gallipoli. Greece, green and beautiful, would have been a vast improvement over North Africa if we had not been hurried north to confront the German Army. In fact few of our corps did much confronting of Germans at that stage; someone had the sense to realize that one division of Australians was useless against overwhelming force, so we had no sooner come within cooee of the foe than we turned and tore south again to take ship for Egypt. There was a short halt, reportedly to make a stand, in the mountains near the famous Pass of Thermopylae, but nothing came of it save that I was kicked by a mule.

As we trooped aboard at Kalamai the Greek civilians watched in silence, not blaming us for not facing inevitable ruin; only an old woman, weeping through her broken English, clasped my arm and repeated 'You will come back, you will come back?' and I said that we would, while the lie burned my tongue for betrayal and my inability to summon enough cruelty for truth.

Some less fortunate than ourselves were landed in Crete, but we made Alexandria in two days, pursued by the Luftwaffe all the way and manning the guns on deck as they came over to bomb and strafe. The psychological situation was peculiar, because on the deck of a ship there is nowhere to run for cover; you can't even disperse widely enough to minimize casualties; you fire back and hope for the best. Between raids groups of us played bridge (contract and chess were the in games that season) and made silly jokes. I doubt that many felt afraid in any conventional fashion; when flight is impossible the mind suppresses useless reactions in favour of a spurious calm.

We went next to Syria; I recall only three days under fire there, though others experienced more. Daily existence there, after the short and sharp invasion, was enlivened by the availability of cheap liquor. Much was undrinkable, but fine monastery-distilled liqueurs could be had at ridiculously low prices; a present-day equivalent might be the purchase of a first-class imported Benedictine for a dollar a bottle. This was war, this was!

The rich drinking holiday was interrupted by a bout of diphtheria, and forty years later a minor, unserious skip-and-jump in my heartbeat was traced to that illness.

Time throughout the Middle East was very much a 'petty pace from day to day', uninstructive because what we accomplished was quickly reversed and rendered point-less. Others took over the business of actually winning and ending the conflict.

With Japan's entry into the war we were recalled home—leaving the Ninth Division beleaguered in Tobruk by Rommel—and I saw my mother for the first time in over two years.

She was in hospital with a bladder complaint, which had necessitated insertion of a catheter, one of a series of ill-nesses that brutalized her last years. It was at first an emotional reunion on her side, one that I made an effort to match, but before the visit was over we were back into the habit of cool appraisal. Nothing had changed.

After a short leave the brigade was sent to New Guinea, which was being invested by the Japanese.

New Guinea in peace or war is an astonishing experience, an island of sensory overload, aquiver with small earth tremors, clothed in a magnificence of forests, burnt by a roaring sun and drowned daily in torrential rain over close-packed mountains whose scarps and canyons stagger the eye.

On the flanks of these green towers, that old description of the infantryman as 'the packhorse of the army' reaches its unstretchable limit of meaning. Nothing before in the way of forced trek in full marching order approached the drudgery of the simplest climb in New Guinea, where every place one needed to reach was either a few thousand feet higher or lower than the start point. In the mud and wet heat, down was little easier than up.

New Guinea mud is unforgettable. The mountain topsoil,

sodden from year's end to year's end, yields softly to bare native feet, but under soldiers' boots collapses into a glutinous trough a foot or so deep; each step is a sinking into black porridge and a slow dragging out. After a while we learned to think not in terms of distance but of 'how long' from A to B, and were not surprised when an hour's striving translated as no more than a mile.

Common sense might reject the idea of a running war of movement under such conditions, but common sense has little to do with it. The soldier is motivated by his awareness of being part of an organism greater than himself; he attempts the outrageous and sometimes the impossible because his conditioning decrees it. He goes *on* because he can do no other; as Childe Roland's road vanished behind him, so the soldier has no way back save in defeat, a word not current in military orders. His existence and his world extend no further than the limit of his vision, which in a rain forest is not far. The wider global conflict becomes hearsay, not relevant to his compulsions. He does what he must.

The Middle East had resigned me to living from day to day, but in New Guinea I came alive. The majesty of the place took my spirit by storm; though I groaned and cursed through the next ten months, I was an individual again, more than a component of a larger flesh. It could be that I was a little unbalanced by this time, but in New Guinea, God help me, I began to enjoy what I was doing. The surroundings helped, but there was a more subtle influence not easily described.

In the open warfare of Africa and Syria you plodded and were shot at, rarely seeing the enemy. It was an impersonal game wherein unseen players picked off pieces at will, an activity with no sense of moving, only of being moved. The rain-forest war was otherwise.

In the rain forest no open spaces made the soldier feel himself a target marked by a watching sky; a clearing with a field of fire was a rarity. There were no spread troop formations with visual contact to sides and rear: there was only movement in single file, often so widely spaced that contact ended at one man ahead and one behind. The desert war was a crackling, whirring, rumbling uproar; the rain-forest war was silent as a bated breath until the moment of contact, when the confrontation was like as not over in a few, bloody, shattering minutes, and the sweating land was silent again.

I loathed the war unrelentingly throughout its six years, but found in that first New Guinea tour a sense of excitement that came close to the *frisson* of an adventure story— that old *Boys' Own Paper* adventure story of the loner loose in a malevolent world. Well . . . there are no doubt times when adventure is a lasting thrill, even when lofted from print to practice, but laced through it is the effort to stay alive to tell about it, and that is the crux whereat the thrill turns sour.

My own souring point was always the rattle of machine guns, which froze my mind and blood. Others found the crash of gunfire demoralizing and still others the earth-lifting detonation of aerial bombs. Of deathful *bêtes noires* there were always enough to go round.

Friendship with Rex ended suddenly when he was killed, not by the enemy but by one of his own sentries. It was an accident of a kind that happened not frequently but frequently enough to shame the trigger-happy, always one incident too late: for some, night in the rain forest, a time of shadows and stealthy sounds, was itself almost reason enough to open fire. Rex's death was a shock but not debilitating; he had been here and was not; life went on; at that time, aged twenty-seven, I had never spared more than passing regret for anyone but myself.

We spent months ferrying supplies over the mountains to build up to the attack on Lae. Native carriers were used but there were never enough for the rush of urgent loads, so the infantry lumped food, ammunition and weapons through the mud and over the razorbacked ridges. Going forward for a month of front-line patrolling became a physical relief.

It ended for me when Colonel Starr decided to send me south to an Officer Cadet Training Unit, remarking that for once he could make an arrangement I could not get drunk enough to break, because we had no liquor in New Guinea. The reference was to an earlier recommendation, which I had aborted with a monumental spree. So I went south and the only bearable stretch of the war years was over.

One of the subjects touched on briefly at the OCTU was the etiquette of the Officers' Mess. Established messes were rare in wartime and nobody warned us that the etiquette can become an instrument of psychological torture in the hands of a dedicated Senior Subaltern (that is, the senior lieutenant of the unit, responsible for the discipline of the junior officers). So, when I reported, with seven others, to take over a platoon in my new battalion, the platoon swiftly became the least of my troubles.

The battalion was one that had spent too long doing garrison work in Darwin, mouldering and unhappy, while other units of the 6th Division were in New Guinea; now it was training moodily on the Atherton Tableland for another New Guinea action, which seemed only a remote promise. There is no life so dreary as an endless fitness campaign.

An Officers' Mess had been set up, run fairly loosely in terms of peacetime protocol but with mind-deadening rigour in terms of the expectations of amateur soldiers trying to not actively loathe their existence. Senior Subaltern speaking: 'The Mess can only draw two bottles of Scotch a month and they're kept for the CO. If he offers you a drink, ask for beer. Have *one* and *don't* offer to return it. Then go away. He's only being polite; he doesn't want to talk to you.'

Sometimes it seemed that the CO, who was a pleasant man if you penetrated the thicket of seniority always clustered about him, did want to talk to us, so that one beer had to last until it risked evaporation in the Queensland summer. I wonder did he know about the Scotch being kept for him? I suspect not; he was a good and gentle man, one of the old school of soldiers who would have fitted snugly into a British regiment; he treated his officers as gentlemen, though few were gentle and a couple were outright larrikins. (A touch of the larrikin, controlled and calculated, makes for successful command in an amateur's war; the men appreciate it.)

Senior Subaltern: 'The Adjutant's method is to sit hard on you blokes and let you come up slowly. That's how it was with us and will be with you.'

The occasional Formal Mess could be endured. Conversation was muted and the raised voice frowned upon; junior officers trembled to the knowledge that any one of them might be called on to propose the loyal toast and in some hideous fashion botch it; no-one could smoke until the Old Man chose to light up; the damned port had to be passed clockwise (or was it anti-clockwise? and who cares?) without the decanter touching the table. Talking shop in a Mess is forbidden and it is ridiculously difficult, in a totally military environment, to avoid breaking that rule. In God's name, what else has a soldier to talk about after years in a warmongers' monastery? No, not that, either; women also are a non-topic.

All this was with gritted teeth endurable for the eight reinforcement officers; other petty annoyances were not.

'Now listen, young Turner, why don't you mix with the other officers in the Mess?'

'I talk to them.'

'Just saying hullo isn't enough. You've got to *mix*. How else will the senior officers get to know you?'

'They ignore us anyway.'

'Only at first. You mustn't push yourself, of course, but you've got to be friendly.'

Quite a proposition. 'Isn't it up to the senior man to be friendly first?'

'That's the wrong attitude; you new blokes are being watched, you know.' The poor man was doing his best not to admit that you were expected to hang round like a puppy with its tongue lolling until some Captain or Major felt like patting your head. 'You don't even *use* the Mess, just bolt your food and run. What do you do with yourself, always in your tent?'

'Read. Write.'

'Write? What, letters? You aren't keeping a diary? That's against regs.'

'Not a diary.'

'Then what?' To my shrug: 'You won't tell me?'

'My private business? No.'

He complained to the Adjutant, who turned out to be quite human when I admitted to being a closet writer of verse and fiction, but felt that I really must be more sociable. Things reached an impasse when after an unpleasantly public scene with my Company Commander I was paraded before the CO, who didn't understand such a thing.

'But *why* don't you get along with your Company Commander?'

'I dislike him, sir.' That upset him so much with its unprotocoled bluntness that I hastened to soften it. 'You just can't like everyone, sir.'

I think no junior officer had ever said such a thing in his hearing; he could find nothing better for me than an avuncular lecture. The OC and I continued to detest each other—and he wore the bigger boots.

I was not alone in rebellion, but my resentment was mostly mute. Four others of our original eight became so fed up with the caste system that they borrowed a jeep, drove to Atherton and loaded it with two nine-gallon kegs of beer. Next morning the officers' lines sported a tent laced tightly closed with a sign outside, OPPOSITION MESS, and four noisily drunken lieutenants inside. What to do with them was an administrative problem when they refused to come out; forcible arrest was out of the question with 800 gleeful privates and NCOs waiting on the scandal. Eventually the battalion was despatched on a route march to nowhere in particular while the problem was solved without publicity—probably by the local Provost Officer and a guard of NCOs. The happy four were paraded before the Brigadier and thereafter vanished from our sight.

For once there had been a grog scandal in which I was not involved.

By the time I saw New Guinea again I was acutely resentful

of the war, the Army generally and the senior officers of my own battalion in particular. Also I was becoming a petty tyrant to my own men and knew it and could not stop.

As a child, as an adult, as a soldier I had never had a confidant; the cool friendship with Rex had produced its occasional burst but never a revelation of any depth, and I did not seek to replace him. My amateur psychiatrist's guess, these decades later, is that I was rebuffing an insistent humanity that might learn to know me too well. I wasn't desperate enough to *want* my soul exposed and punished.

Surliness became open conflict with fellow officers and with my own men; I lost the all-important pleasure in New Guinea itself; the patrolling did not stir me out of a sense of angry futility; I began to neglect simple cleanliness as well as duty. The CO must have been glad to find opportunity to send me south to some unnecessary school, and the decision may have forestalled some really serious upset.

It must be said, in fairness, that the battalion was no worse or better than any other. My dislike was unreasonable and irrational, but so had been all my dislikes since earliest years, rooted in dim mental stirrings that had no connection with officers, the Army or the war.

A few days after I arrived in Melbourne, Japan surrendered. I applied for immediate discharge and got it. That was a drunken day; so was the day after. With the war over, the rational world could await my pleasure for a day or two.

The 6th Division had a fairly quiet war in terms of intensity of experience and time under fire. We did not endure the severe testing of the 9th Division units in Tobruk or the bestial privations of the prisoners of the Japanese; if we struggled in the slime of the New Guinea trails this was, I believe, picnic stuff by comparison with the suffering of our fathers in the bloodsoaked holes called 'trenches' in the Flanders mud of 1914-18.

The horror of Hitler's war lay not in combat but in its

revelation of human degradation and mindless destructiveness. The obliteration of Hiroshima made a startled world hold its breath (for a moment or two) but for sheer horror the firestorms of Hamburg and Dresden transcend it, not in slaughter but in the manner of the slaughter. What has happened across the globe since is enough to freeze thought, to make one wonder if evolution has justified the struggle out of the caves. To know intellectually that violence and inhumanity are the products of desperation and fear is not enough; there are times when the idea of a positive evil loose in the world seems more a reality than a superstition.

It may seem anticlimactic to turn now to the reactions of science fiction to the world's agony, but there is food for relevant thought in that small, self-important corner of literature.

6b
Soldiers and Science Fiction

From 1939 to 1945 science fiction was almost wholly an American product. Other countries were suffering the realities behind the gung-ho fantasies, and their austerities offered little scope for literary fairy-floss.

Only America, despite finally joining the war, had resources to spare for magazines and escapist pleasures. The science fiction magazines were reduced to digest size as a gesture to austerity but their contents were not much affected by world upheaval. The genre had always tended to observe war as a logical outcome of research and 'progress' and rarely paused to examine the implications. Writers favoured armed conflict for its dramatic possibilities but rarely questioned the morality of mass murder in more than a ritual aside. Germany and Japan were sublimated as stellar aliens wading in human blood, their ideas limited to enslavement and murder and their futures limited to destruction by our brave boys armed with blasters (whatever they might be) instead of rifles. The gentle, friendly, civilized alien remained a sentimentalized rarity.

Few of the wartime writers had seen active service, and few who have not been under prolonged concentrated fire can imaginatively create its physical and psychic effects, let alone the real behaviour of fighting soldiers. Worse, the younger post-war writers who had the necessary experience behind them, and knew better, continued to propagate the fictional muscular stereotypes who 'saw red' (a debilitating condition of no practical use), or under terminal conditions 'somehow found the strength for a final superhuman effort' (presumably collapsing thereafter in total breakdown), or, when authorial invention failed, suffered an amnesic spell from which they recovered to find the foe broken and rent during a berserker transport. The readers, of course, were used to this and might have rejected an unfamiliar realism.

Science fiction was not alone in creatively bankrupt nonsense. Most popular fiction projected its war-story elements in much the same style, but science fiction—true to its mind-blowing, star-blazing, cosmos-embracing pretensions—had long ago ballyhooed death into planetary genocide, as if to show that the civilized imagination could deliver pogroms to show Hitler up for a novice. The soldier, as such, vanished as an individual, swallowed up in visions of whole worlds in conflict; there were no recognizable portraits of service men or women.

Not that science fiction offered many 'war novels'; it simply accepted bloody conflict and wholesale destruction as integral to the human future. The writers could and did come up with remarkable technical gimmicks, but their vaunted imaginativeness ground to a halt when required to assess their futures in human terms.

There were exceptions, highly praised exceptions like Kuttner and Bradbury, but they could not alter the popular mask. Sales figures held them in place as an exotic minority.

These thoughts did not occur to me in 1945. It takes time to digest a war, and my literary imagination was still young enough to prefer melodrama to insight. I noted the misrepresentations and shrugged them off. After all, we won—didn't we?

I found that science fiction had become narrow in its interests and something of a repetitive bore, although the biggest names in the business were flourishing and the boom years were not far away; the 'literature of tomorrow' couldn't even observe the facts of its own day and remained, intellectually, a first cousin to the juveniles. The characters were older and nastier, and said things like '$E = mc^2$'.

With such stale dreaming discredited by life, there seemed nothing for me to do but confront the real world of unaccustomed peace.

7a
Short Career

What I have written about the science fiction of the immediately post-war days is not how its practitioners saw it (their attitudes tended towards the messianic) but how it appeared to me in the new dawn when all things should have been wonderful.

Nothing was wonderful.

Having spent my life learning nothing and acquiring no useful skills, I saw, in a rare rush of sense, that men in tens of thousands were about to be dumped on the labour market and that in the competition for work I suffered from near uselessness. I ran for cover to the newly emergent Commonwealth Employment Service and was hired there as an Employment Officer, because I could read and write and clerical types were needed in a blinding hurry.

Unexpectedly I prospered, discovering a talent for fairly rapid interviewing in sufficient depth to keep square pegs out of round holes and perhaps do a little good for the inexperienced and undecided. I stayed with the Public Service for five years, getting promotion, but soon relearning my old routine of operating with half my mind and regarding the hours after work as 'real life'. The Employment Service made little mark on me or I on it.

An unavoidable need was to come to some sort of terms with my mother. She attended a doctor regularly and could no longer work; she did not complain, but her touchy temper became a continuous simmering. There could be no question of our sharing a house, and neither suggested it; we lived in bed-sittingrooms a block apart and exchanged duty visits varied with an occasional night at the theatre. The arrangement worked well enough in averting conflict and when she suggested preparing an evening meal for us in my apartment I agreed. And gave her my spare key.

What I gave her was my peace of mind. She was never out of the place; if I went out she complained of being left; if friends visited she outsat them and blackguarded them when they were gone; if I wanted to write she pawed through the manuscript and criticised contemptuously.

I returned home one evening to find my mail opened and her in a towering fury over some fancied reflection on herself. When I objected to her reading my letters she replied that a mother had every right over the son she gave birth to. Arguing against lost control would have been pointless; I left the apartment and stayed out late, hoping she would have gone by the time I returned.

So she had, and in her own room suffered that night the first of the strokes that soon killed her. She died in a nursing home a few weeks later, at about eight in the evening. By the time I had been summoned, her wedding ring and a small emerald, clung to through the demeaning years, had already been stolen.

In death she was shrunken and weightless but not at all pitiable. Her lips were firm and her soul peered through the shuttered eyelids, refusing dismissal. It was not at first credible that the thirty-year conflict had ended, by default.

She was cremated, as she had wished. My feeling was of relief, of shedding a burden. It did not last.

Turning over her effects I found the notebooks and odd scraps of her diaries. She had not been more than adequately literate; the words halted, the sentences fell apart, the strongest expressions were the clichés of dead melodramas, but she infused them with the intensity of her anger and determination. Hatreds burned and dismays cried aloud; she swore the world might do its worst and never break her. Which is about the way her life went.

For the first time I saw a little way into her heart and

mind, and was appalled for her and at her, and at myself for never having understood.

She had known good from bad, right from wrong, permissible from impermissible, drawing the lines exactly and perceiving no distinctions other than her own. She never understood why her rectitude was eternally punished while those who bent to temptation gathered rewards. She was anti-religious but believed firmly that cheats never prosper, murder will out, fair play begets a fair return, no lie is ever justified, you can know a liar by his averted eyes, children should be seen and not heard and sexual man is a creature to be despised at arm's length. She never understood that her moral stances could command no applause in a world that did not regard righteousness as a practical necessity.

So she was doomed. Her diary told how the world combined against her, how her mother grew to be a mischievous hag and her sister a social-climbing snob, how her father deserted his children, her husband became first a failure and then a moral coward, her elder son wanted no life with her and the younger, 'the brilliant one'—it was there for me to see—had become a mean-spirited drunk.

Indeed she had deserved better than fortune gave her.

If it was a raging against unearned catastrophe, it was also a cry of pain, and its echoes are not yet dead. The furious, astonished vulnerability will not go away. It frightened me because I recognized the same towering, ill-judged, impermeable egotism in myself.

I burned the diary, unable to live with it.

Or so I thought. But the large emotional climaxes tend to fade and be soon done with; reality supervenes before mental balance rocks. Callousness is not a virtue, but breast-beating changes nothing. There may be some point in tears for the ground-down, degraded living—if the tears make a spur to action—but over the dead, even the beloved dead, weeping is finally for the weeper.

Like every pre-damned scribbler who ever heard gunfire I wanted to write my war novel—the narrative to supersede all previous accounts of the fighting soldier. Norman

Mailer's *The Naked and the Dead* brought me down in the slump that followed most enthusiasms; I didn't find his soldiers representative of the men I had known, or even resembling them, or his understandings in any way congruent with mine, but I recognized a powerhouse talent whose existence reduced mine to hand-cranking.

I did not abandon my novel; those were years of confidence and bouncing back. The major characters were set, the initial situation poised for development and my imagination engrossed; I worked and reworked the first 20,000 words, adding a prologue and discarding it, cutting chapters and restoring them, modelling and remodelling the characters. It was a process I was to become overly familiar with; in thirty-five years and nine novels I have never learned how to begin a story cleanly at the first assault. Something like a quarter of a million words must have been expended in getting *Young Man of Talent* over its opening chapters. I still don't like them.

Existence settled to a pattern—eight hours of earning a living, three or four hours of writing each night and a weekend of socializing. I rarely drank during the week (ambition did that much for me, at first) but the weekend was devoted to friends. Call them that; we met only in bars or at parties.

Our drinking stamina was remarkable; those of us who had come out of the war without ruined constitutions were fighting fit. We pitted ourselves now against alcohol, an enemy of some subtlety. That the mechanisms of the body can mesh so long before dislocation is a miracle of biological back-up systems. The brain betrays first; it goes into defence almost at once, throwing up ingenious mental screens to subvert realization that a defeat is ordained; so the body is able to destroy its fine tuning unimpeded.

It is startling to discover how many writers—mainly the less successful—drink like fish. Who cares may draw what inference suits his prejudice.

A small upheaval was on its way. I was good enough at the employment business not to be allowed to vegetate at a suburban desk. Promotions in the Public Service depend mainly on seniority, so that mere proficiency sometimes takes a ruthless beating, but appointments are another matter. As with secondments in the Army, whereby you may be loaned out for a special purpose with a temporarily higher rank and pay, so the public servant can be elevated above his station to a temporary appointment, which can, with administrative cunning, be stretched to the point where he may rise, step by appointed step, to the status of a major departmental figure. (Great can be the fall of one such who puts a foot wrong.)

Nothing so spectacular happened to me, but I was transferred to the relieving staff and set to the taking over of District Offices during the absences on annual leave of their proper senior administrators. It was a boost to the ego, concealing a trap. I arrived one day in Wangaratta, a hundred and forty or so miles from Melbourne and home, to take over the role of District Employment Officer for North-Eastern Victoria. For three weeks, I thought.

The trap was this: My predecessor took his accrued leave and at the same time resigned from the service. I was not concerned; it meant that my stay in a lively and friendly town would be extended for a few weeks while senior men applied for the post. None applied. Facts filtered through, a fairly hard one being that most senior men were married and owned their homes; they were not interested in a shift to the outer darkness. Harder was the pressure applied by Head Office to corner me into taking the job nobody wanted. Head Office won the day by pointing out that if I resigned from Wangaratta there was no other job available at the same level and the Department would be forced (regretfully, as they say) to dispense with my services.

This was 1951, during one of the periodical fluctuations in employment opportunity. I ground my teeth, gave up the Melbourne flat I had been clinging to, and stayed. A little courage at that moment might have paid lifelong dividends. Or not.

What came of this change of circumstances had a touch of the inevitable about it. I blamed the Service for trapping me in the backblocks (though, perversely, I liked Wanga-ratta), transferred resentment to the job itself, gave it the bare minimum of attention, found a solid drinking circle—not difficult with half the male population afloat on beer—and settled to a career of drinking in earnest. My apprenticeship as a weekend drinker was finished; my literary ambitions were shelved indefinitely.

At the end of twelve months I resigned from the Service, formed a business partnership with another drunk, went broke in six weeks, and found a job as an unskilled hand in a local textile mill. I spent eleven years on the factory floor, not unhappy, not really satisfied. At some time I crossed the vague line between 'one of the boys' and 'one of the town drunks'.

In this ambience of decay my literary career began.

Skip the years from 1951 to 1956; one alcoholic descent from cloud nine is much like another.

By 1956 I was forty and frightened. Hangovers, black-outs, memory lapses and fits of screaming temper don't worry the drunk—*lay off it for twenty-four hours and she'll be right, you'll find.* What penetrated the remnants of sense were physical symptoms—dizziness, shaking, crippling stomach pains and sometimes an inability to focus on print. The meshed system was losing coherence under overload.

More frightening was the discovery that I didn't know how to stop drinking. I can't explain that lucidly; I don't really understand it; but any alcoholic will confirm the fact and the fear. The common reaction is to take flight, to somehow get away from the ambience of drink, so I left the hotel I had lived in for five years and rented a bed-sittingroom—then wondered what to do with myself.

Unpacking in the new room I found the chapters of *Young Man of Talent*, abandoned five years earlier, and read them. They seemed better than I had remembered and I thought about taking it up again.

At that time Frank Kellaway was in charge of the Wangaratta Public Library and we had struck up an acquaintance. He had already published some small items and was the only person I knew who spoke the language of literature; he represented all I had lost in leaving Melbourne. Diffidently I asked him to read my half-grown novel, hoping for encouragement but unprepared for his actual response. His 'Finish it' was a command.*

I set myself again to writing five nights a week, picking it up easily after the long break, but weekends I reserved for my drinking company and fancied that stern decision proved something or other.

The novel whose beginning had occupied years of writing was finished in a few months. I bought a second-hand typewriter and early in 1958 had 130,000 words of typescript seeking a publisher. Frank had a literary agent, Carl Routledge, in London and recommended me to him, so off went the baby twelve years after conception; it was submitted to Cassell, who accepted it at once.

To my innocence it seemed a total justification of the determination not to publish until I was 'ready'. Perhaps so, but I had much to learn about being ready. The first fact of unreadiness came with Cassell's demand that I cut 20,000 words from the text. Nearly one word in seven. They surely jested! So much for creative integrity! I hadn't the confidence of a proved success to maintain a fit of temper for long, and a letter from Carl Routledge soothed my artistic pricklings with wise words about the depressed state of the market and the need to cut costs. Twenty-five years later he massages me with the same tired balm; Caxton no doubt used it on his starveling scriveners five centuries ago.

Bleeding at the emotions, I went at the butchery, to discover that not only words but sentences and whole paragraphs could be removed without leaving scars on the aesthetic flesh. I excised 10,000 words and felt I could do no more; this satisfied Cassell, who had probably set a higher figure than they expected me to meet. Aesthetic

---

* Frank Kellaway is a poet and novelist who has no trouble in mixing the life intellectual with the life severely practical, having earned his bread as librarian, farmer, teacher and abalone diver. His liking for my work has never prevented him from seeing clearly the faults that others often miss. He is that rarity, a *useful* critic.

vagueness melted into pride in my new professionalism. I had accepted the implied criticism and completed the work!

A few months ago I read over a few sections of it. Today I could blue-pencil another 20,000 words and end with a better book. But the most ruthless cutting could not make *Young Man* a really good novel. It received excellent reviews (I didn't recognize 'bright new talent' and 'fresh voice in our literature' as tired old critical war-horses) and was bought for American publication (a financial error for Simon and Schuster) but never earned a penny beyond its advances. I don't think it deserved to; it had its virtues—I am still pleased with the handling of the dramatic landscape of New Guinea itself—but the story is not one of them. It is too neat, too perfectly plotted. Army existence is never neat; its sequences are truncated by illness, transfer and sudden death. Now I find the characters too sentimentalized and their psychologies too clear-cut, too clinical. My great war novel was a fine example of how to miss the point.

Friends assure me that it is better than I allow, and the annual Public Lending Right account assures me that it is still read. This is comforting, but the book remains false to its intentions.

And yet, and yet—there is no satisfaction quite like the caress of the jacket of your first published work.

Wangaratta found me mildly interesting for a day or two; some of the locals bought the book for curiosity and made impressed noises; but in a week I was forgotten. It stunted the growth of self-importance. Frank Kellaway was of course mightily pleased at having his judgement vindicated and Hal Porter rang from Shepparton to say pleasant things, but the world was not visibly nudged.

By the time *Young Man of Talent* was published *A Stranger and Afraid* was half written; it appeared in 1961, the work of A Conscious Literary Artist. Luckily for me, no critic noticed this idiot pretension, and the over-wordy book was reasonably well received. *Stranger* still has its readers who think better of it than I do; it needs cutting by a quarter.

Its matter was taken from my immediate surroundings—a country town, an employment office, the intrigues and comedies of pubs and parties. Wangaratta, alias 'Treelake', served me for three further novels, though I had not set out to create a regional series.

The characters were based on real people (*not* Wangaratta people—there has to be some decent reserve), but only loosely. The too, too solid flesh of real people is not sufficiently plastic for fiction; he/she may make a core on which to build but the end product will be far from the original. The plot I let go its own way after setting the characters in motion. I found (still find) this a good way of keeping the story-telling honest, an acting out of the adage that plot is 'character in action'. Authorial interference was kept to a minimum until the point where it became necessary to resolve theme and situation. The catch—every method has one—was that the resolution required weeks of thought and experiment before an ending emerged consonant with the personalities of the actors and not too plainly buttoned and bowed.

Only when *Stranger* was in proof did I face up to a nagging that had bothered me throughout the writing: for nearly three years I had not understood that I was setting out a symbolic mother/son conflict of thumping personal relevance. The mother in *Stranger* was not a portrait of my mother, any more than District Employment Officer Jimmy Carlyon was a portrait of myself (so I thought, though others have pointed the finger), but the conflict in the novel was more metaphor than creation.

She slipped into two later novels, more or less sympathetically, in a placating fashion. Then her ghost for ever investing my work drove me to devise the grotesque mad-matriarch figure in *Beloved Son*. It was unfair and brutal, but I had to be rid of her. She has not troubled me since.

The Cupboard Under the Stairs appeared in 1962. It was a better novel than either of the others, tightly structured and unwasteful. It tied with Thea Astley's *The Well Dressed Explorer* for the Miles Franklin Award for that year. This provided a little money, most of which went on a brand-new luxury-model typewriter, and showed its authority by driving up sales to make *Cupboard* the only one of my novels that has gone to a second printing. Cassell must have at last made a small profit.

Later I came to dislike the book because I had written myself into a plot corner part way through and been forced to introduce an artificial twist to get myself out of it. Ursula Le Guin, reading it many years later, said she could not spot the join, but I know it is there and it rankles, a memory of cheating on my own rules.

Cupboard was completed in 1960, but about four years, twice my normal gestation period, passed before *A Waste of Shame* was finished. Writing had ceased when my weekends-only drinking plan went the way of all half-baked resolutions; by the time the news of the Miles Franklin reached me I was suffering an alcoholic block—not a writer's block but a simple unwillingness to stay sober long enough to write. Add to this a smoking rate of two ounces of tobacco a day (about sixty cigarettes).

One Sunday morning I vomited out my hangover in blood on my landlady's back lawn and collapsed, bleeding internally from the stomach wall. The landlady was at church; I was alone in the house.

I learned this about death: that if there is no pain or fear—and I had never feared it—the going can be gentle. I lay on the summer grass, unable to move or raise voice enough to attract attention, aware of life running down and that I should take some action, but unable to rouse a sense of need. I was dying of loss of blood and my decelerating mind watched the process with interest but no concern. Fading in warm sun with sweat like a cool hand on the forehead is an experience as sensuous as any I recall.

The young boy next door put his head over the fence for one of those non-reasons only the young can evolve, saw the blood and raised the alarm. People fussed; an ambulance arrived; I told them what they wanted to know and was petulantly resentful of their interference. I was *comfortable*. At the hospital they filled me with the blood of strangers, attached a plasma drip, starved me, save for an occasional splinter of ice, for three days, after which the bleeding should have ceased. To make sure they drove a slender instrument down my throat to my stomach and took pictures. The doctor arranged mirrors to let me see for myself. An empty stomach is totally uninteresting.

A mass of scar tissue, they said, liable to bleed at any ill-usage. No alcohol, they said, not ever again. Above all, no smoking. All very sensible; I listened and agreed. It took me four or five weeks to return to my usual consumption of beer and tobacco.

That must have been bravado. I had had, down in the mental depths, a considerable fright, but no Turner ever acknowledged loss of face, even to himself. Death before surrender! Literally.

My mind, cleverer in its subconscious gearing than the simple machine guiding eyes and tongue, played an underhanded trick by withdrawing my ability to 'hold my liquor'. Unpleasant scenes in pubs and in people's homes, plus a humiliating run-in with a normally good-natured policeman, caused me to take morose stock. My two most consistent drinking mates had disappeared from the pubs while I was in hospital and no-one was jostling to take their places; I was very much alone. I suspected where they had gone and made it my business to investigate, to confirm my suspicion. Make a field inspection, so to speak. Alcoholics Anonymous might even make a chapter in a book—if ever I wrote another.

I stayed about a year with AA. It was worthwhile, though in the end I withdrew in boredom with the religiosity and damp philosophizing of the meetings.

I don't propose to debate the virtues and failings of an organization that seeks only to do good. Its first and completely admirable requirement is that the aspiring sobersides must quit drinking cold—no breaking-down period, no tapering off. (Tapering off is nearly impossible, and quitting cold is easier than many a drunk would imagine.) The basic plank of the AA method—though 'method' is a doubtful word for such hazy counselling—is companionship, a friendly support for the ex-drunk who finds himself at a loose end without a glass in his hand. Given good will on both sides it works very well. And often falls to pieces as fast as it was built up.

If the dealings could be kept so simple much might be accomplished, but too many old-timers live in a swirl of righteous sobriety. They can be actively repellent, particularly the neo-religious who claim to have rested their weak wills in the hands of God, and the amateur psychologists who know all about sublimation, transference and the schizophrenic expression of repressed personality. Worse, for me, was the not too subtle insistence on group interdependence, of belonging to a snug little society-within-society with its inevitable undertone of holier-than-thou. Dependence on alcohol was being replaced by dependence on a social sub-system that would soon bore the sobriety out of me.

It was time to leave a group from which I had taken as much as I felt I needed, and a town from which I could expect nothing, time to return to music and theatre, paintings and good libraries and company with intellectual horizons beyond the cattle sales. I gave notice at the mill and returned to Melbourne.

My dues to AA I paid by writing *A Waste of Shame*—an inept title for a book wherein lust usually foundered in impotence. AA loved it; nobody else did. Cassell Australia had taken over my options from the English firm and Bob Sessions, who dealt with the book, was glum about it; the air smelt of publication under protest. The critics backed him up by disliking it thoroughly; one headed his review 'A Resounding Plonkle'.

Despite them, it wasn't a bad novel. It is still strongly held in the libraries, and may well have been read by every ageing drunk in Australia. Its main virtue, aside from a strong plot, was that it treated alcoholism and AA without the greasy sentimentality of sympathy-epics like *Days of Wine and Roses*.

In Melbourne I wrote the last of the four 'Treelake' books, *The Lame Dog Man*. I think it was the best of them, but it made no impact. I remember critical reaction by Tom

106

Keneally's starchy review—for which he later apologized, to my intense embarrassment. The book marked the end of a period; it closed off the 'country town' theme, but no other useful ideas presented themselves.

I took a job as Employment Officer at Volkswagen Australia, vegetating for three and a half years until one of the cyclic motor-trade recessions hit a little harder than usual and a few hundred of us were retrenched—and I lived the truth I had explained across my interviewing desk to scores of still-faced applicants, that at fifty 'we are looking for someone younger, who can be trained for an executive role'.

With severance pay and some casual work I was not short of money, but soon would be. I thought of the Commonwealth Literary Fund, which then fulfilled functions since taken over by the present Literature Board, but lacked a project to submit and was empty of ideas.

Alcohol led to the next step. After a couple of years on the wagon I had begun to drink again, even to get drunk once in a while, but without the compulsion of earlier times, and it was in a pub that I met the ex-boxer whose obsession with his past offered a colourful, ready-made theme. It is a fairly common obsession among sportsmen who were but no longer are; success and peak performance come to them at an age when others are still taking junior steps towards a career, and their vanishment from the limelight is apt to occur suddenly, with youth barely over. Then they flounder in a forgetful world, equipped only with a rusting skill of no commercial value and inner resources never developed.

This pub acquaintance was a savage, railing example of the lost and flailing man and my imagination went to work on him automatically, throwing up scenes and incidents and ancillary characters. The man himself vanished beneath the overlay of ideas; he was only an impulse; there was practically nothing of him left in the haunted and half-mad Cassidy Edwards who finally emerged.

I had my project; the CLF provided funding for a year and I wrote *Transit of Cassidy*.

Bob Sessions was interested in the typescript but

uncertain of the prospects. The reason soon appeared; Cassell Australia had been taken over by Collier-Macmillan and the uneconomic fiction list went with the first sweep of the new broom. I dumped the book and its problems on my long-suffering London agent, who warned me of the difficulty of finding a new publisher without a success story to command attention. He was right. *Transit of Cassidy* lay unsold for ten years.

Disappointment was complicated by a sense of guilt at having taken CLF money for a work that seemed unpublishable; rejection was compounded by a generalized unease at having failed to deliver.

There was no point in carrying on. I had produced six novels, all but one commercial failures, and if I had learned my trade as well as was in me, that was not well enough. The trouble was easily diagnosed: a large ambition and a mediocre talent. It was time to hang up my typewriter, so to speak, and cease piling trivia on the world's stock of forgettable fiction.

That is what I did, taking what comfort there was in the conviction that four of them were reasonably good novels and that the writing had given me great satisfaction. There was regret but no lasting concern; I was learning to take failure, or perhaps myself, not too seriously.

Life, unlike the writer, has no interest in structure or tidy endings; one thing leads to another without form or relevance. While I was being bowed out of Cassell Australia I met one of the firm's sales representatives, John Bangsund, and the science fiction that had receded to a mutter on the periphery of my reading became overnight an insistent clatter. Because of what he wanted of me—a short critical article on the genre—I had suddenly to pay attention.

Science fiction had changed in twenty years; it had not only created the new mythologies that had once been the empty boasts of its writers but had erected a structure of myth about itself. Suddenly it required study.

108

7b
The Career of
Science Fiction: 1946–67

Current fiction had formed only a small part of my reading from the war's end to 1967. I had concentrated on the English-language classics from Chaucer to Conrad, and translations from Homer to Mann. For relaxation I read detective stories and what science fiction I could find.

When in 1967 I assessed what had happened to the genre during these years, it seemed that I had stayed abreast of what mattered. Four major developments had taken place: John W. Campbell's domination of the American field had been broken by editors opposed to his techno-logical orientation; hard-cover publishers had discovered science fiction as a viable commodity; Britain had deve-loped a distinctive science-fictional voice and outlook; and hearteningly, the literary 'establishment' had shown interest in the genre. Despite a general rise in sophistication and literary style, the lowest rung of rubbish was still crowded (as it always is in any genre, that being the ugliest, most commercial level), but the higher rungs were increasingly occupied by writers with intelligence and a willingness to experiment.

Since lines of cleavage were appearing, these topics are best treated separately.

The American Magazines

The 1940s and '50s have become classed as the 'Golden Age of Science Fiction', probably in memory of young enthusiasm; a cynic with an eye on nostalgia has suggested that the Golden Age is twelve. Writers and readers grow old, but the majority readership has always been—despite editorial claims of devoted engineers and scientists—what today's publishers call the 'young adult' and pander to shamelessly. One is reminded of Thomas M. Disch's irritated description of science fiction as a branch of children's literature, though he has done his formidable best to help make it something better.*

'Kiddy lit' may be a fair description of the contents of *Astounding* after the war. Editor Campbell's insistence on a strong story-line (he knew little if anything about characterization and tended to think of psychology as a compartmentalized exact science), coupled with his chauvinist racism, belief in the superiority of scientists and delight in the cunning trick rather than the true value, fathered a line of fiction that proliferates yet. He favoured muscular scientists capable of physical mayhem while their razor-keen brains developed scientific counters to the ploys of arrogant and sadistic foes; aliens tended to be second-class citizens set up for defeat, though some were allowed favourable supporting roles. The stories leaned to ingenuity rather than intelligence but were lively enough to hold the attention.

Campbell's interest in the 'meta-sciences' meant that writers could create a welcome by loading their tales with 'psi'. Telepathy, telekinesis and all related miracles descended on science fiction like a plague, and no cure has yet been found. Nor has any author offered a logical rationale for these mental acrobatics or examined their presumable impact on society.

The eminently sane James Blish wrote *Jack of Eagles* (1952) as a deadpan satire on 'psi' nonsense, stretching its inanities far beyond anything previously published, but his joke suffered the fate of parody that mimics its original too well: the satirical intent was not observed. In any case,

---

* Thomas M. Disch, an American, began his literary career as a science fiction writer, his most important genre novel being *334*, a study of life in the New York tenements of AD 2020. He has also written a witty and hilarious pastiche of the nineteenth-century social melodrama, *Clara Reeve*, under the pseudonym of 'Leonie Hargrave', and some excellent verse.

no-one would have admitted the presence of poison in so profitable a well.

Campbell's well-meant attempt to raise the genre to cultural significance was defeated by his perceptual shortcomings; what he offered as 'adult' was just what the teenagers wanted, high adventure plus the pyrotechnics of super-science, with psi providing the fantasy element. His narrow view of what constituted good science fiction probably *created* the opposition journals. Writers, however intent on producing what would sell, had also their non-market ideas waiting in the drawer, and in-group editors knew of their existence; the opening of new outlets released a flood of 'different' stories.

The Magazine of Fantasy and Science Fiction appeared in 1949 under the co-editorship of Anthony Boucher and J. Francis McComas, a discriminating duo who called for human interest rather than technology; they published stories that preserved a nodding acquaintance with science but were more concerned with psychological impact. *Galaxy*, commencing in 1950, was a little less literary in its approach but featured fairly similar material. Its publication of *The Space Merchants* (under the original, more meaningful title of *Gravy Planet*) in 1952 was a coup of some note; this novel by Kornbluth and Pohl broke out of the 'ghetto' to reach a wider public in many editions and translations. It was, however, one out; conquest of the market did not follow immediately.

The tendency of both these magazines to haunt fringe areas of the supernatural pointed the direction the popular element of the genre was to take. *Galaxy* in fact sprouted a sister monthly, *Beyond*, to fill the gap left by the wartime demise of Campbell's *Unknown*.

New authors appeared, many with original talent—Ray Bradbury, Walter Miller, Ward Moore, Algis Budrys and others—but the readership heroes remained the old faithfuls: Heinlein, Asimov, Anderson, Sturgeon and the rest of the group who had reigned since the late 1930s. These and Campbell continued to give readers the tested recipes. More experimental rivals also found, despite good intentions, what sold and what didn't. By the mid-1960s three

111

or four brands of American science fiction, all energetic enough in production, were entering a new period of stale themes and old approaches. The Golden Age was history.

Hard-cover Publishing

James Gunn, Professor of English at the University of Kansas and a writer of science fiction, refers in his anthology, *The Road to Science Fiction*, to 'the new literature that was neither published in book form nor reviewed from 1926 until 1946'. This, from an academic who has published a history of science fiction (*Alternate Worlds: The Illustrated History of Science Fiction*, 1975), is an unforgivable misstatement. As one who was there to read the works of the period, I have no difficulty in remembering (and checking via the Nicholls *Encyclopedia*) the names of a dozen magazine writers whose science fiction was printed and sold in hard covers. John Taine had at least eight titles on the general market by 1939; others came from such reasonably well-known names as John Wyndham, J. M. Walsh, Edgar Rice Burroughs, Philip Wylie and Ray Cummings.

There was no actual torrent of genre publication, and the reason becomes plain on riffling through the magazines of the time: the hard-cover market took all that was worth preserving, as well as much that was not, and this was a proper response to a fiction often semi-literate and written down to the lowest common denominator of reader acceptance. As for the lack of reviewing noted by Gunn, this was true; critical notice was a disaster happily avoided.

Hard-cover publication became more common after 1946, when the quality was less unbearably juvenile. The first mini-boom began with mushroom publications demonstrating that a public existed; established firms rose promptly to the fast buck. Campbell's enthusiasm, however narrow, had attracted intelligent writers, and such editors as Boucher and Horace Gold had actively encouraged higher standards. Only a few superior talents were in evidence as yet, but some quite good science fiction began to infiltrate libraries and bookshops.

Was it really a Golden Age? The novels that have stood

the test of time are dismayingly few and mostly at the end of the golden limits. There were Walter Miller's *A Canticle for Leibowitz* (1960) and James Blish's *A Case of Conscience* (1958), both thoughtful works dealing with a timeless theme (unexpectedly, religion) as a subject for pondering rather than melodrama, and Algis Budrys's *Rogue Moon* (1960), which used the unlikely gimmick of matter transmission to examine identity in a striking fashion. There was Kornbluth and Pohl's *The Space Merchants*, which, however slickly written and over-smartly plotted, remains a witty and pithy satire transcending its melodramatic frame, and Bradbury's *Fahrenheit 451*, a political satire of great and savage impact. A total of five notable but hardly superb novels in two decades is not much for a genre so vociferous about its virtues.

The ecstatically received fan-reader successes of the period, such as Alfred Bester's *The Demolished Man* and Sturgeon's *More Than Human*, are still read as fresh generations discover the genre, but the older and colder view recognizes them as rickety conceptions that fold at a touch. The huge anthologies launched during the period hold most of the shorter work worth preserving, and five times as much that is not; Ray Bradbury, Cyril Kornbluth, Henry Kuttner and a handful of others gave lustre to the short story, but most relied on ingenuity rather than quality.*

The Golden Age was a time of expansion but now makes little more than a painless introduction to the genre for teenagers. It might be more respected if ninety per cent of the psi nonsense could be excised and buried.

British Science Fiction
The American ability to believe that only American-produced science fiction was worthy of the name ensured that developments in the great world outside the USA would not rock the boat inside it. There was no awareness

---

* *Adventures in Time and Space* (1946), edited by Raymond J. Healy and J. Francis McComas, is one of the earliest of the blockbuster anthologies of the late 1940s and remains arguably the best. Nearly forty years later, it still appears regularly in new printings.

that by 1967 the intellectual leadership had slipped from its grasp.*

From the turn of the century the best science fiction had been written in England, though at long intervals and rarely by authors identified with popular entertainment. By 1946 America had produced no long work to stand beside J. D. Beresford's *The Hampdenshire Wonder* (1911), Olaf Stapledon's *Last and First Men* (1930) and *Star Maker* (1937), Huxley's *Brave New World* (1932), or even S. Fowler Wright's *The World Below* (1929). These were characterized by thoughtfulness and a refusal to sacrifice quality to sensationalism; they were not aimed at an uncritical market but sought recognition among equals.

After some pre-war false starts, British magazine science fiction began properly with John Carnell's *New Worlds* in 1949. He published stories as unmistakably British in tone as those in *Astounding* and *Galaxy* were American; the major difference was made plain by the British writers' interest in the human problems of change and confrontation and by their refusal of gratuitous violence. Carnell's writers did not care who ruled the galaxy or who subjected what to his super-weaponed will; they cared about what people might do and how they might do it. That difference between national products remains to this day.

The roll call of Carnell's writers makes a minor hall of fame: Aldiss, Ballard, Moorcock, Brunner, Priest, Wyndham, Roberts . . . Other magazines of minor quality appeared but Carnell's influence persisted when the limited British market forced the others out of existence. According to Peter Nicholls, in his article on Carnell in the *Encyclopedia*, he preferred 'hard science' puzzles, but in fact he gave space to those 'different' writers—notably Aldiss, Ballard, Moorcock and Langdon Jones—who were to fuel and lead the British New Wave. He did what Campbell was incapable of doing in America: he trusted not

* As late as 1975, Professor James Gunn could write in his anthology *The Road to Science Fiction* 'Even today science fiction must seem American in order to feel like the real stuff.' So much for academic and critical perceptiveness!

114

only his personal taste but also his critical judgement of quality outside his taste.

In 1964 Carnell retired from the editorship of *New Worlds* in favour of Michael Moorcock, and the New Wave of British science fiction finally broke. Writers concerned themselves with the inner world of the human mind (though *not* with psi potential) rather than the universe of atoms and galaxies, and so were forced to abandon old techniques in order to make statements requiring fresh forms. Their impulse—to shed the constraints of a genre showing signs of age—was sound; they had worked too long for a pittance to submit to the straitjacket for ever. Led by J. G. Ballard, and soon followed by Moorcock and, less flamboyantly, Brian Aldiss, the revolution began.

There was initial confusion among readers. Fresh directions they could welcome, but when plot receded into the background, when language and form became matters for manipulation and obtrusive techniques dazzled clarity off the page, they were not always willing to give the careful attention asked of them. In a career too colourful to relate in detail *New Worlds* alienated the escapist readership but reached new areas of the literate, including academics. Moorcock brought speculation to science fiction, rather than extrapolation, taking the logical step forward from the base laid down by Verne and Wells. And he succeeded in bringing sophistication to style and content. The extrapolative base did not disappear (why should it?) but was assimilated and regurgitated in new forms, while the speculative impulse spread through the writing community. British science fiction was never to be the same again.

Not all that Moorcock published was good; much was minuscule thought dressed in narrative technique to ape significance, a commonplace of literary revolution, where readers and editors lose their way in the avalanche of novelty. When the sifting begins, the charlatans fall through the mesh and the writers remain. Old names vanished, often to reappear on the American market, and young ones, recognizing the rise of *their* mode of expression, came to the fore. Scarcely a genre writer was left unchanged or unimproved by the New Wave experience; even the formula writers learned and profited.

This was not the end of the story, but by 1967 its influence was assured.

An American New Wave

The parallel American evolution had a different beginning and a different ending. A number of highly individual writers haunted the scene after the war's end—notably Ray Bradbury, Kurt Vonnegut and Alfred Bester—but no general movement formed around them, though many authors were restive under editorial restrictions. These were imposed partly because of the youth of most magazine readers, who might turn cold to the attention requirements of experimental fiction, and partly to placate the Middle West morality of those later known as 'the moral majority'. Sex was carried on behind curtains of metaphor and symbol.

The increase in hard-cover publication, reaching a more extended and literate public, made it possible for a few authors to bypass the magazines, but the magazines were still the main market, assisted by specialist paperback houses, which followed the proved magazine formulas; innovative writers, when unexpectedly popular, were special cases whose example one could not risk following.

America lacked a Moorcock to head a revolt and work himself into the ground to keep innovation viable. So, when the Moorcock *New Worlds* appeared in 1964, the attention of a few American writers was aroused sufficiently for them to offer him, despite the comparatively beggarly British rates, works that could not find a home in the USA. The most spectacular of these was Norman Spinrad's foullanguage melodrama, *Bug Jack Barron*, which drew much comment but has always seemed to me one of Moorcock's errors of judgement, a singularly pointless novel celebrating four-letter speech but little else. More importantly, writers like Thomas M. Disch and John Sladek found Britain receptive to stories that followed the New Wave interest in the problems of 'inner space' but retained their distinctively American tone, the hard-edged expression that contrasts strongly with British smoothness.

In time, other American writers sought wider freedom,

with Ursula K. Le Guin and Joanna Russ bringing new honesty to the depiction of female characters and sexuality generally; but where the 1964 New Wave became the whole ambience of British science fiction, in America it was seized on by mass-market writers for its outspokenness and no-holds-barred imaginativeness, producing a fiction of technical virtuosity and aggressively free expression that was fundamentally the mixture as before in a fresh wrapping. Even freedom of sexual expression was won for a time in the tide of cultural mores, but has lately been lost again in a new swing towards moral righteousness. In Britain the New Wave changed the face of the genre; by 1967 it had, in America, only added—apart from the work of a few genuinely dedicated writers—new gimmicks for mass-market scriveners to exploit.

Informed Criticism
The Golden Age authors who complained that their novels were not accorded critical notice should have been glad of it. Honest treatment would have been merciless.

The genre developed its own network of in-group reviewing in hundreds of 'fanzines', most of it inept, ignorant and postulated on the basis of 'If I like it, it's good; otherwise, it's awful.' But there were some intelligences at work, and one of them, Damon Knight, became the first in-group critic of note. As a competent writer and editor his concern was with the content of stories as well as with their presentation, and his more scathing comments revealed many writers as logicless ignoramuses and purveyors of nonsense for money. It is probable that he achieved little in a basically juvenile subculture and was read as much for his sprightly skewering of pretension as for his attempt to bring order to a disorderly genre. His magazine reviews were collected as *In Search of Wonder* (1956) and they give a vivid picture of the wilder idiocies of the early post-war period.

Another American, James Blish, writing as 'William Atheling Jr' (and once or twice using the pseudonym to review his own books), took up Knight's torch and commenced a crusade of 'mainly technical criticism'—his own statement of his intention in a letter to me. An Atheling review must have been a traumatic experience for some of the self-satisfied prolific and careless, but he used a skilful technique of dissection to reveal not only failings but the values of superior work and their significance in social and cultural terms. His essays (*The Issue at Hand*, 1964, and *More Issues at Hand*, 1970) were less spectacular than Knight's but more useful to the intelligent writer and reader.

By 1960 reviewing was a feature of most professional science fiction magazines—but their criticisms had only the force that might be expected from in-group writers reviewing each other without questioning the conventions and limitations of their medium, using 'stunning' and 'magnificent' freely enough to price genius at two cents a pound. In-group criticism came close to communal back-scratching. Uninvolved commentators were badly needed.

It may have seemed that these were at hand when in 1959 the English Department of the College of Wooster, Ohio, fathered a critical magazine, *Extrapolation*, but it was not so. The journal's blandly academic concentration on bibliography and studies of the generic past rendered it useless to all but the thesis student. Items were examined but not the broad field.

In 1967 this was still the general state of the art in the USA.

In Britain a more viable impulse came, with the impact of surprise, from the academic side of the critical fence. In 1960 the novelist Kingsley Amis, then a lecturer in English at Swansea, brought out *New Maps of Hell*, a collection of essays on science fiction. It was an unsatisfactory survey, concentrating on those satirical and anti-cultural aspects that fed Amis's own literary interests and misconstruing much that seemed to him of less importance, but it was an influential book. Within the science fiction fold it was welcomed as bestowing some general establishment cachet, though its conclusions were hotly and rightly contested, but the name of the author of the best-selling *Lucky Jim* was enough to earn *New Maps of Hell* an audience beyond the science fiction ambit. The style of the work was not portentously scholarly but it spoke to the intellectual as well as the fan; in England and Australia it did more than any previous writing to make science fiction culturally acceptable. A respectable number of academic fans emerged from their closets to add a friendly word.

So far so good, but the situation was far from satisfactory; acceptance and a body of informed opinion are not achieved overnight.

PART TWO

THE DREAM-WORLDERS

8
A Dweller on
the Fringe of Fandom

One enduring result of my meeting with John Bangsund
was that my daily existence became to some degree involved with science fiction and has remained so. The
device of parallel chapters can be abandoned.

Says the adage: One door closes and another opens. What
John Bangsund opened to me, as my career came to its
unnoticed end, was more like a mousehole, but it led in
time to a second career.

John, then in his late twenties—solidly built to the point
of being only slightly higher than wide, recusant from an
uncompleted seminary training, *bon vivant* by inclination,
belletrist by avocation and exquisitely literate by sensitive
predilection—was in his spare time the editor-publisher of
a privately circulated magazine, *Australian Science Fiction
Review*, usually called *ASFR*. As a member of staff with
Cassell Australia he had noted an incautious reference on
the jacket blurb of *The Lame Dog Man* to my liking for
science fiction, and filed it as an opportunity target.

He introduced himself, spoke of *ASFR*—and would I
care to write something for him? It may not have been
quite so quickly done but memory insists it was. I agreed,
and the reason must have been rooted in a lightly stroked
vanity; John specializes in softly persuasive manipulation,
nothing so vulgar as flattery bùt achieving the same marsh-
mallowing effect on the prey.

With a few sample copies of *ASFR* for reference I began

my education in the anthropology of an entire human sub-group, Science Fiction Fandom.

Fandom—without headquarters, hierarchy, constitution or agreed reason for existence—is a world-wide non-organization such as only undiscriminating enthusiasm could have generated and only an undying enthusiasm maintained.

It seems to have been born in the 1930s, possibly by way of the pulp magazine letter columns, when extramural correspondence sprang up between letter writers sympathetic to the ideas of other letter writers, and to have snowballed tremendously after the war. Though an essentially youthful phenomenon, fandom has a solid centre (including many writers, editors and publishers as well as ageing readers) that has maintained involvement over four or five decades.

Fandom cuts across social barriers of race, language, nationality, colour, ideology, financial status; even comparative literacy and general intelligence become totally assimilated in what is not so much a subculture as an *idea*, which has penetrated every major country in the world. (Perish any thought of world-wide harmony: fan groups, each with its own version of the *idea*, can feud it with the best. Melbourne and Sydney, for instance, preserve little more than impolite recognition of each other's existence, and in Scotland I caught an impression of Glasgow fans regarding themselves as beleaguered among non-Glaswegian groups.)

The non-organizational aspect is central to a freely fluid community and attempts at organization in the past have been strongly resisted. Most groups do not have club rooms or regular meetings, but individuals circulate in continuous socializing, so that each fan is always in loose contact with dozens, possibly hundreds of others. Even the conventions, where several thousands forgather in the vast American get-togethers, are run by committees formed for the occasion and disbanded when the job is over. So fandom is a *social* phenomenon, cemented by unusually intimate communication between comparative strangers.

Prominent fans are known to each other in an international camaraderie. A well-known fan, or even one not

124

so well known, could be passed from hand to hand completely round the world, from Australia and back again, should he make use of this pan-global good will. But how does one become a 'prominent fan' in this unintegrated milieu?

By publishing a fanzine, or writing for one.

The word 'fanzine'—literally 'fan magazine'—has found a place in the dictionaries and needs no excuses from me, but a more precise definition is not simple.

A fanzine will be published by any fan who wants to correspond with other fans or who simply wants an audience for his thoughts. It may be only a couple of roneoed or photocopied sheets stapled together and mailed out every month or so; again, skipping a thousand intermediate gradations of quantity and quality, it may also be a sophisticated journal running to many thousands of words of original material, provided with original line drawings and photographs; the most ambitious publications may be offset printed, with colour artwork. Distribution may be local among a score or so acquaintances who exchange issues, or it may run to thousands of copies read around the world. (France, Germany, Japan and the Scandinavian and South American states are among the most thoroughly saturated non-English-speaking countries.)

Most can be ordered for a price calculated to barely cover costs; nearly all operate at a loss. The larger fanzines may be open for subscription at around two dollars a copy (and may be worth it) but can lose money on a daunting scale for their producers; short print-runs and petrifying postal charges put hope of recouping costs out of the question.

Why individuals should undertake such costly and labour-demanding tasks is a question for psychologists, but writers, publishers and readers are quite overtly conscious of participating in communication on a plane atilt to the relationships of conventional living. Most *live* reasonably conventional lives, but within fandom they speak on a freer, more personal level than with their everyday contacts. As to *what* they communicate, the spectrum is limitless. Science fiction may once have been the core

125

subject, but this long ago gave way to more personal interests. Most treat science fiction and fantasy—if they treat of them at all—as peripheral; their pages are filled with editorial ramblings on any subject to hand and with letters wholly concerned with personal foibles, travels, fan contacts and the airiest of chitchat.

There exists, however, a hard core of large-sized, literate, stringently edited fanzines aiming at professional standards, concerned with science fiction and its literary relevance and filled with criticism, publishing news, author interviews, theme essays and so on. There are not many of these, but they are the main forums for non-academic discussion of the genre.

One such, in 1967, was *ASFR*.

The word 'fanzine', with its built-in hint of amateurism, is not good enough for such journals as *ASFR, SF Commentary*, the American *Locus* or the British *Arena*. These are 'little magazines', filling in their erratic fashion a literary corner rarely noticed by establishment journals. Less scholarly than their more dedicated prototypes, they are also less committed to the publication of solemn ephemera wherein bibliographical reference too often takes the place of original thought. They are well informed within their limited area and written with an *esprit* that makes them entertaining to read. It *is* possible to be lively, amusing and seriously informative within the same frame of words.

These amateur publications have attained reputable standards. Literary figures who command respect outside the genre (Stanislaw Lem, Brian Aldiss, Tom Disch and others) have donated articles and written letters of comment to the major Australian fan editors—and on the intellectual side have taken the occasional towelling from correspondents lacking the servility to accept their pronouncements as law. Fandom is not respectful of age, dignity, wealth or reputation.

John's sample copies of *ASFR* contained surprises. I had not expected the sophistication, which alerted me that tossing off some trifle would not do in this company; the standard of John's own prose—urbane, witty, even a little deliberately precious—was a challenge to my straight-forward style. Looking for weakness, I found it in the review columns, where books were praised, damned and mangled by fans who knew what they liked but had no conception of critical aims and standards. I had never reviewed a book in my life but felt that I had the technical knowledge (I had, but less than I thought) to launch an attack on inept criticism, and coldbloodedly set to work to reform the art.

Beginning in callow arrogance, the crusade didn't deserve to succeed, yet in a fashion it did.

With weak criticism the heaviest millstone round the neck of the genre (there is ground for argument that it still is), the useful thing to do was to take a stand for excellence. I chose one of the most highly praised science fiction novels of the period and subjected it to some four thousand words of clinical dissection. Nothing like icono-clasm for waking sleepers.

The object was not so much to expose Alfred Bester's *The Demolished Man* as a jerrybuilt novel as to expose the critical vapidity that allowed it to be praised as a work of great significance on the strength of virtues it did not possess. It was an expert thriller, a scintillating exercise in high-powered story-telling, but the brilliance was obtained by ignoring science, psychology and common sense; far from having intellectual content, it was a fine example of literary sleight of hand, with action too fast for the reading eye to observe the trickery.

'The Double Standard' was the impertinence of a self-appointed shepherd telling the sheep they couldn't recog-nize the real nature of their forage, but reading it fifteen years later, the only change I would make would be the deletion of an undeserved sneer at J. G. Ballard. I have pursued the sport of hunting inflated reputations ever since.

John commenced my career in science fiction by pub-lishing the article in *ASFR* 10 for July 1967. Others followed and I found myself a centre for cheers, catcalls, furies, staunch supporters and others who would have had me turning over a slow fire. The vehemence of the fan

127

reaction shook me to the point of wondering if I had started more than I could follow through, but I had not then learned that fandom operates only at the top of its voice, sound and fury signifying little more than a zest for polemic. A letter from Robert Bloch (known to the big world as author of *Psycho*, but to the fans a fellow fan), praising the Bester article, stiffened my spine for the commission of a far greater impudence.

In *ASFR* 18 appeared 'On Writing About Science Fiction', a piece of rash didacticism laying down the law for reviewers and critics: how they should and should not view the genre, what they might and might not say, which critical attitudes were and were not permissible. This act of self-advertisement should have raised the hackles of every critic in the business; rather, it made me known across the science-fictional globe. James Blish conceded that it was 'excellent', no small accolade. Fanzine publishers in England and America sought permission to republish it—the most recent just two years ago. I would prefer it buried. It says nothing I would wish unsaid (though there is much I would wish to add), but says it so badly and baldly that I cringe at the recollection. Still, it gained me an audience outside Australia.

At home, personal contacts with fandom were less successful. Some regarded me as a disruptive force; also there was a generation gap, which I made no attempt to cross since there are few pretences more fatuous than middle age aping the attitudes of youth; again, I was not and am not a gregarious type. I met a number of the leading Melbourne fans of the day and found them more intellectually aggressive than other literary groups—more aggressive than knowledgeable. They were, in that decade of cool rejection of the past of their parents, old enough to be clear-eyed in logic while young enough to be touchy and ill-informed in matters of aesthetics and judgement, and suspicious of all criticism as an assault on their values. They tended to bore a personality too socially careless to give a damn for their values and too out of touch to sympathize with their desire to change the directions of society. They knew their subject—themselves—and I didn't.

Some of the more consciously intellectual were hard to take. I met John Foyster and Damien Broderick, a pair of fairly ferocious mentalities, and found their conversation so allusively remote as to constitute a shutting out of the intruder. I gathered that they found me uninteresting, but times change and we with them, and we all know each other much better now—sufficiently to disagree profoundly while yet finding each other's brains worth the picking. On the whole I was—and am—uneasy with fandom, unable to enter its enthusiasms.*

In 1969 John was tiring of *ASFR* and branching into more personalized publications, so Bruce Gillespie and his *SF Commentary* dropped neatly into a slot ready to receive them. I began to write for him.†

SFC became something of a fannish sensation, penetrating America and England to such an extent that the labour of production became excessive and over-expansive. But the quality of contributions attracted attention; work flowed in from Stanislaw Lem, Franz Rottensteiner, Ursula K. Le Guin, Philip Jose Farmer, Philip K. Dick, Brian Aldiss and dozens more; the signatures in the letter columns were enough to turn a young fan's head, but the backbone of the journal remained Australian.

The local talent had come a long way in the three years since John Bangsund had begun demonstrating the virtues of style, and the standard of reviewing, though still confused, had shed many early crudities. I was prone to flatter myself as a standard-bearer in this respect, but the truth is that many others, notably John Foyster and Bruce Gillespie

* John Foyster is a Melbourne educationist whose attitudes and opinions, allied to hard work, have had a lasting and beneficial effect on the general directions of Australian fan activities. Damien Broderick has published several science fiction novels; he took over from me in 1982 as science fiction reviewer for the Melbourne *Age*.
† Bruce Gillespie is an ex-schoolteacher who advanced via fanzine publication to professional publishing as a partner in Norstrilia Press. His 1983 volume, *SF Commentary Reprint Edition: First Year, 1969*, is a startling testimony to the improvement in fanzine standards during the three years since John Bangsund aimed at quality in 1966.

himself, were by force of example demanding more intelligent criticism. I only made a noisy splash in a stream already flowing, but I was receiving a sufficiency of pats on the back to ensure that I enjoyed myself with my new hobby.

Self-satisfaction, earned or only assumed, was due to be shattered in ludicrous fashion, but to appreciate the flavour of the joke it is necessary to look at another aspect of growing up.

Speaking with Damien Broderick one day during the writing of this book I mentioned the difficulty of settling the truth of experience, of the uncertainties involved in recovering attitudes of mind in lost years—particularly assumptions regarding the attitudes of others—and the care needed to ensure that the involved and still living are not caused grief by the upheaval of truths they were unaware of. Autobiography is a self-indulgence that should not be used to inflict pain; a complete autobiography would be an act either of masochism or of vengeance.

Damien thought, naturally enough I suppose, that my reference was to sexuality, for most of us have a destructive item or two locked in that classified file. He pointed the commonplace that sexuality is not a slice of life that can be swallowed and then ignored but a nourishment of what we are and do. I forget what I answered, because I was at once preoccupied by a perception that could not be delivered until it had been given some thought: that this generalization might be less than accurate, and that the sexual life is often less a formative factor than a reflection of the manifold other aspects of a personality, not so much a conditioner as another conditioned aspect.

There are men and women aplenty, more of them each generation in a sexually 'liberated' era, to whom the once horrendous public traumas of marriage and divorce are no more than a twitch in the skin of their self-obsession, and there is no need to home in on prostitution in order to see sexuality as often no more than a simple tool of transient indulgence. Man is the beast that has broken the sexual cycle, and in consequence learned to subject sexuality to other needs and often to subsume it in them. It is not enough to speak of love and desire with the assumption that both terms are implicitly understood; they are understood in the mind of the speaker but translated into other apprehensions in the mind of the listener. We know less about each other's meanings than we think.

All these sinuosities do not save us from sexual guilt, which runs deep and does not recede with time but surfaces sooner or later among the terrors of recollection. I do not mean remorse, that useless breast-beating over irrecoverable fact, but the guilt proceeding from the knowledge that time after time you have betrayed the image you presented to the world—and to yourself—as the admirable you. After sixty or so years the past becomes an attic of ghosts gibbering their astonishment that with an iron selfishness you once committed this act and that, never taking account of the core of self-knowledge that sits grinning in vengeful wait.

These were the ideas I had in mind when I cut short the conversation with Damien.

Three things about sexuality as it affects this essay in time travel: First, the narrative includes only those matters that seem to me to have direct bearing on the themes laid out in the first chapter; whole areas of aesthetic experience, working life and personal contacts are merely summarized in the interest of continuity, or simply excluded. Second, I belong to a generation that considered sexual experience a matter private to those concerned; we were certainly wrong in this and we carried a social convention to dangerous and destructive lengths of secrecy, but such intense conditioning dies hard. Third, it is not my business to deal out publicity to one-time partners under a specious guise of saintly truth; no names no pack-drill, says the soldier, and I have no desire to double round the parade ground of eternity with the psychological blood of others spattering my steps.

There were, of course, too many women in my early life. The only lasting male influence in my first twenty-three years was Alfred Floyd; both father and elder brother vanished without becoming properly established in my mind. It was inevitable (this is hindsight trying to make order of what at the time seemed casual experiences) that the young man's treatment of women should be compounded of wariness of a lifetime's authority figures and a determination to break free of them. The outcome was a coldbloodedness hard now to credit.

The 'mutual chemistry' theory of sexual attraction was popular in the 1930s and it suited my needs very well, setting all contacts in a 'scientific' context and recognizing the emotional element as transient and deceptive. So one could indulge safely in a grand passion for a week or two and return to reality—and fresher game—with a philosophical 'C'est la vie; she'll get over it.' In most cases she probably did, being no more deeply engaged than I.

There were two exceptions, one a case of quite relentless desertion and the other of moral cowardice; I don't propose to dwell on either. What concerns me now is the ability of that self-obsessed young man to ignore guilt. These episodes took place during war-time, when the shucking off of responsibilities was easy in view of the more urgent problems to be faced in the field. But wars end and we live to deal with our pasts.

Guilt did not in fact surface until in middle age I at last formed actual friendships with several women and had to recast my view of the sexual balance, to get rid of the symbols of repression and rage. (I tried to embody the change of attitude in my writing at the time but was pretty clumsy at it.) The great irony is that this occurred towards the end of my alcoholic period, when the physical effects were at their height, and it is a miserable truth that alcohol stimulates desire but kills performance stone dead. Regard it, if you like, as punishment-by-denial for former brutalities, but the real smack in the teeth was still to come.

I was over fifty, squarely in the fabled land of middle-aged madness, and I was due to trudge every inch of its salt-sown desert. For the first time in an egocentric existence I fell in love, as distinct from the more familiar 'in passion', which feels much the same but wears away to less traumatic endings.

And having written that, I stop to wonder what I really did fall into, aside from Alice's treacle well. 'Fell in love' is meaningless; love is built over years, not minutes. 'In hypnotized idiocy' fits the facts.

The story is the classic stuff of sexual Snakes and Ladders, involving a married woman, her husband and besides myself another man (who eventually scooped the kitty), and investment in a business that never got off the ground. To this day I find it difficult to think of the insane web of double dealings with rational detachment, but if, as some sadist has said, there is good to be found in everything, it can only have been in teaching me that I was capable of stupidity on the grandest scale.

At the end of it I was ill, frighteningly depressed, stripped of everything I had owned (including most of my acquaintance) and several thousand dollars in debt.

One friend whom I had managed not to alienate asked me, as he might have asked of a naked fugitive, 'But what will you do?' and I said 'Start again. Start a new career.'

That was bravado and I suppose he knew it. His incredulity told me how I appeared to him—tipping into old age, broke, jobless, shabby and shattered.

I wasn't shattered; there was infinite resilience at work; there was also a need to absorb what had happened, to understand the vanities involved and review the world with a few more illusions discarded. Still, the career-building boast was at first an empty one; the need was to rock back to stability.

I took a job as a factory hand with Carlton and United Breweries, rented a furnished room, and lived like a rat in a hole for twelve months until the debts were paid. Then it was time to start again.

133

9

Ragged Edges

I scraped together enough money—to the devil with debts for a week or so—to buy a second-hand typewriter. It was a rickety, collapsing machine whose immediate product was an article for *SF Commentary*, a quirky, sputtering review of the science fiction that had appeared during my absence from the fannish scene.

Science fiction, a necessary frivolity to balance austerities, became unexpectedly a supportive sideline. John Bangsund was by then working for the Melbourne *Age* and he convinced Stuart Sayers, the Literary Editor, that he should accept me as a casual contributor reviewing science fiction. The money put occasional jam on my bread, but the boring truth of the reviewer's job hit at once—that it is one thing to be aware of the existence of a ninety per cent junk content in current fiction and ignore it, but quite another to be required to read the junk and write intelligently about it.

In my first year I rejected about half of what I was given as unfit for serious consideration. Of the rest, Le Guin's *The Left Hand of Darkness*, Lem's *Solaris*, Abé's *Inter Ice Age 4*, Dick's *Ubik* and a couple of anthologies represented all that was commendable; in 1970 science fiction was still the preserve of ageing hacks, though some new names were promising better. Regular reviewing, with restricted choice, is not only work but boring work. The only way to justify writing about garbage-in-garbage-out fiction is to write honestly, and that is enough to erode your faith in creativity. You begin to understand, with the bitterness of revelation, why others have dismissed your own work with scant respect.

I doubt whether, after thirteen years, Stuart Sayers and I really understand each other's ideas about science fiction. He did not pretend to know the genre or to want to know. The field was mine; his not to interfere. Politely, he never said outright that the stuff was a waste of intellectual time, but the thought teetered on the edge of exposure. When I floated *Brave New World* as a trial balloon for literary respectability, he said 'But you don't call that science fiction, do you?' and was mildly shaken by my assurance that I did. There is no dialogue when two people speak the same language from different reference points. Confining ourselves to neutral ground we got along smoothly enough and he gave me a fair amount of 'mainstream' fiction to handle as well as such non-fiction, mostly popularized science, as he felt came within my range.

The column, once a month on average, kept strained finances in bearable check; I began to refurnish my vanished library and disorganized mind. If I had in 1967 ceased to take myself too seriously as a writer, by 1970 I had come close to refusing to take myself seriously in any way at all. Once the attics of self esteem have been cleaned out they look barely fit for habitation; best not to consider too high-flown a restocking.

Writing a science fiction novel was not something I had consciously intended, but several pressures combined to direct me to it. Not the least of these was John Bangsund. It is unlikely that he ever said anything so crude as 'Why don't you write a science fiction novel?' That is not his method. Chances are that he closed the trap on some innocent statement of mine, such as 'If I were treating this theme I wouldn't take such a headlong approach', and thereafter professed to assume that I had announced the subject and mode of a work about to be commenced. The next step would be a bland 'You haven't anything actually on paper yet?' with the effect of starting up guilt feelings, followed at intervals by throwaways like 'Do you find your suggested approach viable in practice?' It is the good-tempered, water-drip method of infinite patience, which succeeds or drives mad. It may not have been applied in just that fashion, and John's own version is restricted to a shoulder-shrugging 'Can you blame me for trying ever so gently to nudge him in the direction of writing the stuff'—but it happened.

Critical dissatisfactions probably played their part. The New Wave writers were doing interesting things but also, in the 1970s, inspecting their aesthetic navels rather than the matter of their conceptions, too often delivering technique by the cartload with only a flaccid and lifeless fiction stirring at the end of the working day. Little of that ferment has stood the test of the few years since. I wondered what would emerge if, instead of deciding 'I shall write a science fiction novel on such and such a theme', one reversed the procedure to say 'I shall write a novel in which the science-fictional element is crucial but still only one of several'. I felt that the science-fictional statement might be swamped by characterization and structural considerations—but there was the gemlike example of *The Hampdenshire Wonder*, wherein nothing was lost, to be pondered. It was necessary that the work should not forsake the genre's huge imaginative vitality, but it was equally necessary that *people* rather than mere characters be brought back into focus. I wrote essays hammering the point; nobody was impressed. (Gene Wolfe, Tom Disch and Christopher Priest were still feeling their way.)

A goad came from fan reaction to my abrasive essays, a healthy resentment of what was seen as arrogant dismissal of fan interests and preferences. The fans were not wrong, but their anger—a real anger, attested by a couple of cases of personal abuse—expressed itself mainly in fanzine letters asking 'What science fiction did this so-and-so ever write that he claims to judge his betters?' This variation of the old schoolboy taunt 'If you're so clever why ain't you rich?' is not one that should trouble the honest tradesman, but in fact if it is repeated often enough it gives rise to a self-questioning: 'Am I indeed so competent?' The answer is 'At least more so than my detractors', but the thorn has pricked, and rankles.

Searching for a theme, I concluded that few major concepts had not been exploited to the edge of boredom.

Since I had written often enough that all these had been mangled into melodrama without thought of factual possibility or social consequences, I had no option but to re-examine one of them with an eye to more realistic treatment. For me the game must be played within the rules of reasonable possibility—no mind-blowing for sweet mind-blowing's sake.

I began a pilot exercise with half a dozen people in a homing starship—emphasis on characterization, with possible plot points noted in passing—and a parallel group in a post-holocaust Melbourne, neither group in contact with the other, but approaching confrontation.

At the end of a few months I had the confrontation but no idea what should happen next. Such blank-wall stoppages have been endemic to my method of creation—what the characters did next must be what they reasonably *would* do, given their natures and circumstances. Here the difficulty was to select those actions, from many possibilities, that would satisfy the general intention of the theme, while at the same time building around them a new social and technological system without reducing the action to spasmodic jerks. It was the first of many stops and starts. The writing occupied about four years, on and off, with one major interruption when my life stumbled into its next reorganization.

In the brewery where I spent forty hours each week doing nothing that taxed brain or muscle I was one who did not drink on the job, not because of reservations about alcohol but because drinking would have involved furtive collusions. My job was solitary, in the cellars; I liked it that way; a taste for self-sufficiency dies hard.

Nor did I drink much outside the brewery. Still, when Christmas of 1972 came round, and it was party time in fandom and everywhere else, I went to several powerfully alcoholic gatherings in the week between Christmas and New Year—and on New Year's Day came to grief.

The party was at Robin Johnson's flat and was the standard Australian party—too many people in too small a space.* A non-standard item turned out to be myself.

In a week of circulating I had probably drunk more than in the previous year and was also insulting my stomach with cigars. I arrived at the flat already awash in gin after a day of casual fraternizing, with a small gut pain that was not subsiding as it should under the caress of alcohol. John Bangsund was present; I was talking to him when the pain increased suddenly to the edge of what I could bear without doubling over. My abdomen swelled and stiffened but I retained wits enough to understand that an ulcer had perforated, the stomach contents were leaking into the peritoneal cavity and that again I was on my way to dying.

I don't know what demon of cock-eyed calmness takes over at such times, but I reckoned that I had several hours in hand before internal bleeding killed me, that a thoughtful person should not make a fuss and destroy the enjoyment of others and that home was only two blocks away. I made my excuses with a fine display of insouciance and asked John to drive me home, which he did. It seems not to have occurred to me to tell him what was wrong or sensibly ask him to drive me to the nearest hospital. So he dropped me off and returned to the party.

Inside, I sat down on the hall carpet and could not get up again. The phone, two yards away, was for ever out of reach. I thought myself alone in the house but a woman lodger had come home early and, hearing the collapse, came to investigate; she had not only had a New Year drink but had prepared for bed with a couple of nembutal. Myself clutching at pain while trying to explain what I wanted to a lass too fuzzy to read the directory properly or to find the numbers on the dial must have been laughter for the gods, who are partial to black comedy, but our combined efforts at last produced an ambulance. I had a sense of time running out faster than I had calculated, but a cheery ambulance attendant assured me that I hadn't

---

* Robin Johnson is a globe-trotting Australian fan (without benefit of a personal fortune) who knows everybody in science fiction and is liable to be encountered, heading for a convention, anywhere between Heard Island and Novaya Zemlya.

perforated anything, that he had seen it before and it was . . . Whatever it was, I made my point by emptying a stomachful of gin, supper and blood over his uniform. He settled for urgency. At the hospital I passed out.

When I woke in the ward my head was unexpectedly clear, my ego self-satisfied (well, I'd made it, even if on the deathknock, hadn't I?) and my stomach constricted and tender. During the morning I learned that I had been so close to DOA that the theatre staff had gone straight into exploratory surgery without X-ray, removed the wreckage of the ulcer, sewed a flap of stomach wall over the hole and put me to bed.

'*Not* a neat job,' tut-tutted the very young surgeon when he visited. '*Hurried*, you understand.' I understood. 'You were very lucky.'

'I'm always lucky,' says I, arrogant in the face of fate evaded. It was true: I have had the Devil's own luck not to finish in a dole queue, in an asylum or on skid row.

In three weeks I was out, with six inches of brilliant purple scar from sternum to navel (that exploration really had been hurried) and inexplicably cured of smoking. After the enforced abstention in hospital the desire for tobacco never returned; a thirty-year addiction vanished without any trace of the psychological symptoms complained of by heavy smokers deprived. What had happened (in hindsight) was that the stress problems that fostered an addiction had vanished; I had suffered not only another brush with death but a fundamental reorientation to living.

Tracing a reorientation is difficult; there is no consciousness of change in the moment of its happening. The mind alters direction without informing the awareness, which continues undisturbed as though debilitating pressures had never existed; it cannot chart the moment or the reasons, only assess the result. Several months passed before I saw that during the stupidity of that last collapse I had shaken off some mental shackles.

In a closeted and repressed childhood I had imbibed a grossly distorted view of the social world; as an adult I had suffered the consequences. I think that when I joined the army at age twenty-three I had the social outlook of a twelve-year-old; when I left it at twenty-nine I had attained the attitudes of a school-leaver, for the crude social pressures of a wartime army are astonishingly similar to those of a senior school. Life thereafter had been a struggle to have understanding catch up with my age in years; there had always been pressure to cope, more maturely than I could manage, with situations that seemed irrational or demeaning.

What now developed was a decision to live without explanation or apology, to be guided by common sense and my own predilection, to break with throttling social pressures, to fall in with convention when it suited me and refuse when it did not—to in fact make my own decisions about what I owed to acquaintance and convention. It meant dropping many pretences, ceasing to fake interest in transient contacts or to suffer fools with a pleasant smile, or to do what was expected of me by those with no right to expect anything, or to be eternally available when I preferred the privacies of my choice. These are the common pressures to which most of us pay resentful toll, and they are deadly.

I thought I might as a consequence lose a few disposable acquaintances, temporarily distress a few friends and gain a name for aloofness. These things happened, but in the long run my circle grew larger than it had ever been. Let others psychologize on that; I only record that life offered wider satisfactions and there seemed now to be time to take serious interest in music, film and theatre, all neglected for too long.

There is a sardonic touch in fathering these contentments on New Year over-indulgence and an inane flirting with extinction. Is there after all something to be said for the idea of 'good in everything'—if you can survive to observe it? Luck is a useful accessory.

By the time I had finished *Beloved Son*, in 1975, the science fiction scene had changed again. In England the New Wave had survived the splash of stylistic experiments, most of them gone out with the undertow. What remained was an invigorated corner of literature whose cousinship to the science fiction of Campbell or Gernsback was many times removed.

J. G. Ballard had come through a period of raging surrealism, fired by personal bitterness, into a round of sociological metaphors—*Crash, Concrete Island, High Rise*—related to the genre but not really of it. Aldiss had demonstrated pyrotechnic versatility with *Report on Probability A* and *Barefoot in the Head*, neither representing his deeper capabilities, and returned to a more straightforward manner; his facility for operating in any current style left him sometimes suspect of being merely 'up with the latest', but in fact his view of the possibilities of a mutating genre had broadened and his most progressive period was beginning. Moorcock had completed most of his influential Jerry Cornelius novels and their offshoots, as well as his bread-and-butter heroic fantasies, and was seeking greater space for intellectual manoeuvre. Christopher Priest and Keith Roberts had made initial impact, and a number of competent but less original novelists were holding the popular line for the common reader without resorting to lowest-common-denominator tactics—among them Bob Shaw, James White, Michael Coney—while Ian Watson had become, with *The Embedding*, the British shooting star of the early 1970s.

With the self-conscious revolt quietened and calmed, the natural leaders began the real work of probing the limits of the genre. But once the limits are passed, is the result still science fiction or something totally other? The question will surface again.

Whatever the answer, the British consumer front had stabilized after a period of semi-indigestibility; the new modes had found assimilable form.

In America the death of John Campbell in 1971 had loosened the leading-strings but changed little in his private empire; the severely technological story now belonged almost wholly to *Analog*. More freely ranging work, in so far as it had a magazine base, was fostered by *Galaxy* and *Fantasy and Science Fiction* and a new public was being drawn into the fringe areas. Important as writers, in or out of the genre, were such subtle emergences as R. A. Lafferty, Gene Wolfe and Thomas M. Disch—but the rumblings of Frank Herbert's phenomenal success with *Dune* were already heard and the time was near when vast, unwieldy, oversized and confusedly written tomes would dominate the market, following a trend in hugeness, commanding enormous publishers' advances and selling in hundreds of thousands. The science fiction boom was on its way, and a literary boom brings with it formula fiction processed to public taste so long as the dollar rings up sales.

In America as in Britain quality was appreciated by those able to recognize a fine text and left to rot by the majority, who used science fiction—meaning bizarrerie and dreams—as a shot in the psychic arm.

And in Australia? Very little in Australia. A. Bertram Chandler had been writing his popular Grimes/Rim Worlds tales for many years, but these carried only the occasional hint of country of origin; Chandler is English by birth and not wholly to be claimed for Australia, though he has lived here for many years. Promisingly, Damien Broderick had published a novel and a collection of short stories in local paperback, and Wynne Whiteford and Frank Bryning were writing the occasional short story as they had done for many years, but there was no general movement that could be called Australian Science Fiction. John Baxter was able to compile two anthologies for Angus & Robertson (*The Pacific Book of Australian Science Fiction*, 1968, and *The Second Pacific Book of Australian Science Fiction*, 1971), and though the *Second Pacific Book* contained much stylish work, its better content was drawn from fringe areas that did not cohere in any fashion.

Plenty of youngsters wanted to write science fiction, and did so, thrusting much of it on me for criticism on the understanding that a professional writer must be willing to give his time and experience free of charge (most of us are, in some degree, God help us), and nearly all of it was hapless rehashing of the contents of the current overseas magazines. It seemed that the only worthwhile science fiction produced in this country would remain M. Barnard Eldershaw's *Tomorrow and Tomorrow* (an underrated work that deserves more than passing attention) and that little originality could be expected.

One always hopes to be wrong about such judgements,

and I was wrong in looking to the burgeoning British scene for inspiration and impulse; it came instead from America, in the visit of Ursula K. Le Guin as Guest of Honour of the World Science Fiction Convention in Melbourne in 1975.

By 1975 Ursula Le Guin had written most of the science fiction of her early career; *The Left Hand of Darkness* had roused my enthusiasm in 1969 as the only balanced feminist statement in science fiction, and *The Dispossessed* (the best ideological meditation in the genre) had repeated the effect in 1974. She came to Australia at the top of both fan and critical popularity, admired and wondered at and collecting awards from all sides—all of them deserved, itself a matter for remark in a venue whose award-giving often defies comprehension. She was an obvious choice for Guest of Honour and a momentous one.

Ursula Le Guin, raised in an academic environment, a Fulbright Scholar with a master's degree in Romance languages, married to a history professor, is hearteningly down-to-earth in her literary approach and possesses the gift that distinguishes teachers from instructors, the ability to establish instant rapport with a class. She showered it on a pre-Convention writing workshop in the hills outside Melbourne, where twenty young and unpublished Australians, all urgently creative, attended what became for them—their accounts attest it—a magical week.

I visited the class one morning to discover how a writers' workshop operated (also hoping like any excited fan to speak with a writer whose work gave me pleasure) and saw that Le Guin's secret lay not in what she did but in what she is. She inspires enthusiasm without working at it. I had done a fair amount of specialist teaching over the years (not of enough importance to clutter this chronicle) and recognized the psychological Midas touch. In that week in the hills she justified every cent of what it cost the Convention committee, backed by the Literature Board of the Australia Council, to bring her to Australia; she transmitted not only knowledge but heart to young writers who had no local market for their work and needed a Grail to follow. Nearly all of them have since been involved in the development of an Australian science fiction as writers, editors or publishers.

The true value of her visit was given before the Convention opened, and there is no need to write of that. Conventions are for fans, for the reverent touching of the garments of the currently revered; they serve to keep enthusiasm at white heat. Le Guin contributed more to Australian science fiction before the junketings began than have the whole total of star-strewn conventions since.

Her influence encouraged the launching of further workshops from which promising talents have emerged; it encouraged Norstrilia Press (also founded in 1975) to drop a fannish ambition to publish essays on science fiction and turn to science fiction itself, beginning with *The Altered I*, a volume of stories and essays written by the Le Guin workshoppers; it initiated the habit among young writers of originating ideas and treatments instead of grinding out pastiches of the stories in imported magazines, and this was the most valuable residuum of her visit. The idea of a personal attitude toward their writing, divorced from English and American models, had rarely occurred to them as a viable approach and they came to it gingerly, without much understanding of what was involved. But it was a beginning.

The visit of Ursula Le Guin provided a focus for my own not at all modest ambitions. I decided that if I could exert any influence at all on the local science fiction scene, it would be devoted to fostering an Australian idiom in this foreign field.

10
An Innocent in
Science Fiction Land

The obvious first step in the promotion of an indigenous idiom was publication of a successful indigenous novel, but from the first I was doubtful about the probable reception of *Beloved Son*. It expressed views unpopular in science fiction readership about such traditional warhorses as telepathy, utopias, cloning, political organization and the like. The readership is basically conventional; it wants and for the most part gets 'more of the same', and this I had not provided. (Why bother to fire, in 1975, the outworn artillery of 1945?) Worse, I had discarded conventional linear plotting in favour of thematic development, asking for sub-textual understanding and arriving at a downbeat conclusion. Most science fiction readers, say the polls, are young, and the young prefer optimism; looking at what they face today, who can blame them?

Still, somebody has to stand for iconoclasm, so off went typescripts to Carl Routledge in London and his opposite number, Howard Moorepark, in New York. Here are their immediate reactions—and who wants to be a writer must learn to stand firm against many such:

> Dear Mr Turner,
>
> I have read *Beloved Son* and am sorry to say that I do not think it would be saleable here—apart from being twice as long as a s-f novel should be. In my opinion it moves slowly, cumbersomely, and the characters are so dim that I couldn't find any of them interesting enough to care. It goes back to you by sea mail. I'm sorry.
>
> Sincerely,
> Howard Moorepark

What hurt most was: 'the characters are so dim'. I had banked heavily on three or four of them having enough intrinsic interest to carry the reader through the thematic intricacies.

Carl's reaction, gentler, was no more encouraging:

> I am sorry about this. I enjoyed reading the novel, but then I am in a special position vis a vis yourself . . . all my desire is to like it. But that doesn't alter the fact that it is . . . a long, slow read, and you need your wits about you. I can't imagine the Woolworth's readership going for it, next door to Asimov and Moorcock on the SF shelves, can you? . . . try for publication in Australia.

I had recovered well enough from the Moorepark clubbing to observe clearly what was said. Both agents noted the length of the book (150,000 words) as a strike against it—at a time when the really long science fiction work, up to 200,000 words, was swamping the mass-market sales. Carl's reference to Woolworth's made me suspect that the problem was less the book than the salesman.

Every writer needs an agent and most writer-agent relationships are long-standing and friendly, but it must be remembered that each agent forms for himself a working base consisting of a core of successful writer-clients and the publishers who buy their works; inevitably he tends to specialize in the fiction field that forms the bulk of his operation and may be out of his depth when a hitherto dependable author presents a typescript that doesn't fit the expected parameters. My agents, in fact, did not know the insular science fiction enclave.

Feeling better for this rationalization (a reasonably correct one) I insisted that the book go to John Bush, who handled the large science fiction list at Gollancz, and myself forwarded the other copy to Harper & Row in New York, mainly because they had the good taste to publish Ursula Le Guin.

> Dear Mr Routledge,
> I am afraid we cannot make an offer . . . Basically it is far too long for its own good . . . for my taste a

lot of the long dialogues about philosophy, sociology, science etcetera could go . . .

    Yours sincerely,
     John Bush

Since these 'long dialogues' were the core of the book, what should I do with the remaining three or four pages? Safer not to ask.

Harper & Row sent a bland, formal letter of rejection—an informationless dismissal telling the writer nothing about the reaction to his work.

Perhaps I had indeed strayed beyond my limits. Gollancz and Harper are not cheapskate houses; they have prestige and standards; rejection by them carries some connotation of mediocre performance. Yet I knew myself not incompetent and that the decisions of the most experienced judges are open to query. With mulish determination I took stock of my finances and decided to take my 1976 holiday in England and scout the literary terrain for myself. Besides, I had always wanted to see London and had never before been able to afford the trip. I was fifty-nine; there was still time for new places and new experience.

Lee Harding had just finished editing his science fiction collection, *Beyond Tomorrow*, for the ill-fated Melbourne house of Wren. It was a good collection and he asked me to deliver signed copies to some of his English pen-friends, including Brian Aldiss and Christopher Priest as well as another editor, expatriate Australian Peter Nicholls. Expansive with anticipation of England, I said, *Yes, yes, of course, of course.* I was to wish I had refused.

I landed at Heathrow with a sketch map and instructions for finding the house of the friend with whom I was to stay. The instructions were on the lines of: *Take a taxi, get out at X and the arrow is home. The fare should be five pounds.*

The fare was about ten pounds. When I protested against being taken for a colonial halfwit the cabby detailed, extempore and without taking breath, a list of 'extras' to be legally included in the take. Not knowing the local rules, I paid up. It was almost worth the few quid to see a trouper go into his act with all stops out and never a false note—pavement theatre at its best. No-one in England again robbed me so blatantly. That I know of.

My Australian host, Brian Thompson, a schoolteacher with some clout in educational circles, launched me on a cram-course sampling of London, with little freehand diagrams showing how to find important places, such as the Covent Garden Opera, in what we think of as back lanes. I saw most of the obligatory London in spite of a tendency to linger in magical corners of the British Museum or gossip with an affable gorilla in the Regent's Park Zoo when my schedule said something like National Portrait Gallery. (The dullest art gallery extant. Avoid it.) Best of all, I attended all I could of British theatre, which is totally exciting. Then there was the London to be seen by wandering the streets, looking and hearing and smelling, the only way to enter into an environment.

But this isn't a travel book; it is a book about—well, partly about my education in science fiction. I picked up a lesson or two in England.

First I rang my agent, Carl Routledge, who offered me lunch at the Press Club in Fleet Street. It is a famous club, but then everything in London is famous, or behaves as though it is. Carl turned out to be about my own age, with a general appearance filed erratically in my mind as 'retired colonel'. (Will that shock him? I wonder how he pigeon-holed me?) The manner, however, was neither colonel nor retired; people face to face do without the euphemisms and atmospheric flourishes of correspondence, and we got smoothly down to business.

He had two novels, *Beloved Son* and *Transit of Cassidy*, that he could not place and I agreed to take them off his hands and try them with Australian houses. This was not wholly truthful on my part, but I was not about to tell a man with ten times my general experience in the trade 'Listen, mate, you just don't really know the science fiction scene', if only because I didn't know it either, but meant to play a long shot with *Beloved Son*.

I didn't want to antagonize Carl nor have him feel over-borne; he had looked after me for twenty years with little return to himself and had even had *Transit of Cassidy* retyped when the poor thing began to fray from handling by too many publishers' readers. A hundred thousand words are not typed cheaply, and I owed him more than the common courtesies. In any case, I didn't know what to do about *Cassidy*, which had hung fire for a decade, other than heave a despairing sigh.

I set about delivering Lee's books. Finding Peter Nicholls was not difficult, and he took me to meet Hilary Bailey. She was editing *New Worlds* in the closing issues of its career, so we were all able to commiserate on the condition of literate science fiction.

I remember Hilary as the only British science fiction writer without an aura of constant watchfulness against unfavourable reaction to his/her work. We writers are a tiresome lot. The Australian breed is aggressive about less than complete agreement with his own assessment of his work, while the British are self-consciously defensive; only the Americans seem capable of dealing comfortably with something less than hero worship, though those who aren't can be appalling. Writers should be permitted only cautiously to fraternize with people, never with each other.

The next delivery was to Brian Aldiss, and this went badly from the start. Part of the reason was my social clumsiness and bad temper. He lived outside Oxford, which meant the expense of a whole day of my crowded twenty-six just to hand over a parcel. While I cursed this wasteful commission, Brian Thompson suggested that I might save the day by looking in on a fine Uccello in one of the Oxford galleries; worth the trip, he insisted, and I pretended to agree.

So I rang Aldiss and decay set in at once. I explained, with sublime crassness, that I wanted to see the Uccello and this made a good opportunity to deliver the book. He said 'I think that's pretty insulting' and I realized too late that I had trodden the *amour propre* of a man very conscious of his eminence in British science fiction. His eminence is deservedly great, but the truth is that writers rarely interest me as persons and I saw no reason why I as

151

a passing tourist should interest him, and what I had seen as a simple commission was assuming the trappings of a Great Man pilgrimage.

I have never been noted for split-second recovery but I made some sort of placatory noise that gained me an invitation to lunch. More time wasted, I thought gracelessly, but was not in position to refuse without real boorishness.

So on the morrow I went to Oxford, was met at the station and proceeded to add injury to insult. Aldiss's story in Lee's anthology was 'The Oh in Jose', a pleasant, average Aldiss piece; casting about for a comment that would be complimentary without fulsomeness, I suggested that the treatment was reminiscent of Somerset Maugham and that Maugham would have appreciated the theme. I was made at once conscious of error; Maugham was not a suitable comparison. (Maugham has suffered critical downgrading and can now be safely repudiated by those who learned their trade from him; the verdict of time may yet be a slap in the teeth of his detractors.) With straight face and malice aforethought I shuffled mentally through possible alternatives and came up with Robert Louis Stevenson, who has been back 'in' these last ten years or so. He was approved. Rather meanly I counted coup on a private scoreboard.

Aldiss gave me lunch at a hotel where we dined in the open air beside the river. The food was good but the conversation less than easy, with both of us something ruffled. I took myself off at the first opportunity.

I located the Uccello and was sufficiently out of sorts not to appreicate it as I did on a later visit; I returned to London conscious of time and contact wasted by my own fault. Starting on the wrong foot, I had never managed to change step. Aldiss can be charming and witty company but I had given him no chance. He can also be damned difficult; so, alas, can I.

He remains a driving force in British science fiction while his major contemporaries, Ballard and Moorcock, have moved away from the central stem.

Christopher Priest was next on my delivery list; he lived then in Harrow on the north-west edge of London. We had exchanged a few letters earlier in the year (it was now June) and I was determined this time to make the effort to meet him on proper terms of give and take.

Chris had made a splash in the previous year with his novel, *Inverted World*, which turned out to be his last foray in genre science fiction. His new book, *The Space Machine*, was written at something of a tangent to his previous output, but it was not until I read *A Dream of Wessex* (1977) that I understood the nature of his dissatisfaction with the genre and the line his thought was taking. Like so many who can be clear in print, Chris is not easily graspable when he tries verbally to define the ambitions that are really only expressible in the form of the work that proceeds from them.

When we met again at the Writers' Week of the Adelaide Festival in 1982, he was still able to say little more than that he wanted 'to open up the genre', expand its limits . . . We all say that, and God only knows how many different things we mean by it, but in 1982 his novel *The Affirmation* was available, telling more of his intention than anything he could have said. The book is neither science fiction nor fantasy nor quite *sui generis* . . . There, I have become as vague as he. He is one of those people—rare, I think—with whom some personal acquaintance adds to the understanding of his work. With others it often confuses. So, in terms of satisfaction, this meeting paid off for me six years later.

A quotation from one of his letters is apposite: 'Priest Dictum: "The true subject matters for writers to discuss are money, sex and beer".' He is probably right, but the disgraceful truth is that we discuss other writers, often with fangs barely concealed; our appetite is for gossip. From every editor, writer and publisher I met in England I absorbed in-group scandal, mostly hilarious, often malicious, little of it less than bitchy.

I suspect this is true of all in-groups. Not among the virile working classes, you think? Well, I worked among them for twenty years, and it's an education to hear those quiet, reserved types on the subject of their fellow tradesmen; the step from the workbench to their bedroom secrets is about a sentence and a half long.

I don't pretend to be above the battle. Writers, despite

ivory-tower image-building, are the same flesh as their readers. How else could we write of them?

With the chores done, I went to Scotland for a week, mainly because a friend in Australia had sung the praises of Edinburgh as 'having the whole smell of history about it', an unusually evocative phrase from a plain-spoken man who himself hailed from Glasgow.

He was right. To walk the mile or so of Canongate, from the eagle-crag of Edinburgh Castle to the dour silence of Holyrood, is to tread a thousand years of blood, treachery, high romance and murder.

Edinburgh, like London, fascinates as a museum of a people's past, weltering in tradition and pride, but is really a Sunday-best display case. Curiosity took me to Glasgow. Ex-Glaswegians regard their city as something between a tragedy and a bad joke, swearing they will never go back there; other Scots mention it with gentle forbearance, as for the family drunk they can't do much about. Even the ticket-seller at Edinburgh's Waverley station, recognizing a tourist, asked 'Now, why wad you want tae gang there?'

I replied: 'I'm Australian; we're eccentric.'

'Ay,' said he, acknowledging a fact.

The central sector of Glasgow is horrible, hemmed in by the shells of deserted warehouses, windowless, boarded up but bearing the small signs of furtive occupation by the fugitive and penniless. You see poverty almost as soon as you step from the train; it takes time to discover Glasgow as one of the world's great repositories of Victorian architecture, a city of much magnificence if you seek it out.

In three days I conceived an affection for Glasgow and its people. They are friendlier than the Edinburgh folk and much friendlier than the English, who seem always to be considering the limits set by good manners and their sense that foreigners should be handled with care. I felt at home in Glasgow.

Being like all scribblers parsimonious of experience, I left the city already mulling over its possibilities for a

154

future fiction. Writers hoard their lives, minute by minute, against the day of need.

Time ran out. I would take *Cassidy* home with me, but the Australian market did not promise much for *Beloved Son*. What little science fiction had been published there had been, with too few exceptions, poor stuff that had profited nobody. I needed a British publisher.

I fixed on Faber and Faber, partly because of its standing as a major house with names like Golding and Kazantzakis on its list (the horseless beggar might as well wish himself among bloodstock) and partly because it had published Aldiss and now Priest. In that house a novel whose mode and structure stood a little to one side of the science fiction norm would at least be appraised with intelligence.

I called at the Faber office on my way to the plane, left the typescript on the reception desk with a covering note to Charles Monteith and walked out with a sense of boats burning glumly behind me. Four blunt denigrations from those on whom my hopes had rested were poor company for the flight home.

Charles Monteith's highly appreciative letter of acceptance followed me in a matter of days.

It brought relief rather than elation. It might seem that I had proved two agents and two publishers wrong, but that would have made amateurish rejoicing. That some like a certain book and others don't proves only that tastes differ and, in the case of publishers, that policies vary from house to house. That your book is accepted means only that one firm sees commercial possibilities in it. With a house like Faber and Faber it means also that your work meets an acceptable standard of literacy and intelligence; neither of these is essential to popular success, nor does their presence guarantee favour from the reading public.

Nor need a publisher's letters cheer the novice unduly. His enthusiasm doesn't really put you up there with Graham Greene and Patrick White; it is his business to stroke your ego if he wants another book from you. The author knows nothing about the prospects until his book is published and the critics have had their meal of it.

With publication scheduled for 1978, I had eighteen months to wait. An author with proven sales potential may be rushed into print but the rest wait until a favourable position on the sales list can be found. Considerations now were the sale of American rights and British paperback rights. The paperback rights went to Sphere almost at once, but I was not sanguine about the US market; in terms of American popular fiction, terms very different from those of the British market, I had contravened more guidelines than enough by failing to observe any at all. The novice who is not aware of US guidelines must be quickly made so; sex, structure, length, profanity, theme and a dozen other matters are subject to the rules of different firms; until he achieves some market success and with it a measure of liberation, the novice's hopes of American publication belong with process work rather than literature.*

Hope of hard-cover publication in the US was faint, and I was happy to see the book picked up by David Hartwell of Pocket Books, a paperback subsidiary of Simon and Schuster. Like Monteith he was enthusiastic and the money was good by Australian standards—for those who wonder what the prizes are like, $10,000—more than I had earned from all my previous books. Grasping at chance, in 1977 I said a metaphorical *To Hell with slavery*, resigned my brewery job and became my own master.

Being your own master is entirely practicable so long as you are prepared to put up with the consequences. I knew at the time that it was a risky move and also that it was then or never; there's a limit to doing totally unintelligent

---

* Some US publishing firms base their science fiction programs on library sales and find it necessary to have in-house censors to hunt down Dirty Words. In 1981 I had to find substitutes for such comparatively mild words as 'shit' and 'screw' in a story, 'A Pursuit of Miracles', written for a Terry Carr original anthology. The Moral Majority, it seems, sniff out such abominations like truffle hounds, and insist on the offending book's removal from all library shelves. I'm not sure that our local brands of wowserism aren't preferable. On the other hand, a writer driven to make such changes soon discovers that it is quite possible to achieve the necessary impact without four-letter assistance. Dirty Words are often no more than a lazy writer's cop-out.

work for the sake of creature comfort and this was the final step in my hospital-bred revolution. I would spend my life doing the things I wanted to do.

Decision was brightened by an unexpected sale to the Dutch paperback firm, Prisma. The possibility of German or French translation rights had occurred to me (Chris Priest had found them profitable markets), but neither was offered. I learned in roundabout fashion that the 150,000-word length made translation, which is very expensive, prohibitive with an untried author. This is understandable, because good translators are rare, but the small Netherlands market found it practicable and was able to show a profit.

All these transactions promised pie in the sky, but there is no way of really estimating the fate of your book or your pocket. It is safer, with the money in the bank, not to expect much more. Most of us sit sensibly behind our typewriters, tapping out fresh hostages to fortune; we can't waste precious time envying the gold-showered, best-selling one half of one per cent of writers.

The resuscitation and short life of *Transit of Cassidy* filled part of the waiting time. It had its comic element. I entered it for the Alan Marshall Award, mainly because I couldn't think of anything else to do with it. The judges placed it second, which soothed the ego but provided no cash; *Cassidy* seemed still in transit to nowhere in particular.

Then came one of those twists of circumstance we call luck, for want of a better word. Thomas Nelson Australia, who financed the Award, were not interested in publishing the winning novel (which was picked up by another firm) but wanted *Cassidy*. The letter telling me this was signed by Bob Sessions, the one-time Cassell editor who had given me the news of its rejection eleven years earlier. He called me in for discussion and I wondered, as I wonder still, if he remembered dealing with it before. He gave no sign and I let the depressing history lie.

He wanted cuts, said it was diffuse at some points and needed tightening. It was a complaint in that foggy area of criticism that leaves the writer unsure what is expected of him. Technical criticism, I replied, should be precise—

chapter-and-verse stuff. Bob possibly recalled similar heckling in the past and was ready for me. He opened the typescript at a marked place, put his finger on a paragraph and said: 'That sort of thing.'

I saw straight away what he meant—rumination, commentary, authorial intrusion, which took the reader's attention from the main matter. You don't often get so exact a statement of what is wrong, or so sensible a conviction that you will, once alerted, yourself see that it is wrong. Science fiction workshoppers get some good training in this; most professional reviewers are hopeless. Between technicians little argument is needed; that is a useful part of what professionalism is about.

I took the book away, made the excisions—a whopping 5000 words of ill-fitted padding—and in due course it was published. The anecdote should end in triumphant financial success, but in fact *Cassidy* dropped dead. The critics liked it and the library borrowers liked it, but no public queued to buy it, nor did it find a paperback publisher; the sweet smell of success is apt to last about two days in the fiction business and the fate of nine-tenths of published fiction is instant oblivion. It is hardly possible that the uninvolved should understand why writers persevere with the odds stacked irreducibly against them. The writers themselves don't understand why. The creation of fiction is less a profession than a compulsion.

11
Living with
Reviewers and the Trade

So your novel has been published. *'O frabjous day! Callooh! Callay!' / He chortled in his joy.* This chapter is about what happens next.

Readers tend to favour a 'dependable' reviewer, meaning one whose taste marches closely with their own, but have little idea of the tiger-infested reviewing arena, where the finest books are as liable to bloody dismemberment as the worst. Years may pass before consensus on a book's merit takes shape, but the judgement of time is of little use to a writer seeking the bubble, reputation, and a living.

The fledgeling novelist confronted with a dozen reviews of his book may be dismayed by the mechanics of butchery. He will find his plot mangled, dialogue misrepresented, theme misunderstood, characters misinterpreted and most of what he thought valuable disregarded—all this by a reviewer bent on praising the work! He will find, in another paper, every point accurately understood and assessed, with a final paragraph suggesting it's a pity such diligence could not have been applied to a worthier end. He may wonder desperately if some of the less coherent reviews may have confused his book with somebody else's.

After a week or two of approaching each new notice as if it may draw a pint of his blood he will realize that most of these reviews are neither as deadly nor as unreasonable as at first they seemed, and that it is quite possible for contrary summations to be extracted from the same data. He may even admit, sourly, that if the book is misunderstood the fault may be his own.

Beloved Son, addressed to a different audience from that of my earlier books, was for practical purposes a first novel. The chilling reaction of agents and publishers' readers has been noted, as also the enthusiasm of the eventual accepter; what was to come was infinitely more bewildering. English publication preceded Australian by three months, as did the reviews, so I knew the best and worst before it arrived here, but only nerves schooled to utter indifference could fail to respond to this:

> . . . a huge chunk of world-mothering creativity, a damp gust bringing rain to the waste land of British SF . . . as I read it I could have clawed myself for pleasure . . . On the laughable assumption that literary awards and prizes were based on merit, *Beloved Son* would collect a whole slew in '78.

All that in the one review in *Newsagent and Bookshop*, a London trade paper with some influence on the ordering of booksellers! I was immensely bucked but had been in the game too long to imagine there would be many notices like it. Nor were there.

Birmingham Post: '. . . his writing style is so flat as to be dull . . .'

The Guardian: 'Mr Turner needs a few gaffing lessons from Mr Pohl . . . it's a relief to turn to George Martin's *Dying of the Light*.'

Alex De Jonge wrote in *The Spectator* that 'it reveals a profound sense of politics'; Couze Venn, an Oxford don writing in *Foundation*, denied me any sense of politics at all, or of anything else for that matter.

And so on. All in all, the English notices, most of them by reviewers outside the science-fictional ambience, were very good; only the *Birmingham Post* gave an unequivocal thumbs down. My assessment was: Good enough throughout to ensure sales to the libraries and go some way toward ensuring that the print-run sells reasonably well. It would be some months, the fan world being what it is, before the

160

in-group amateurs got to work on it; their reactions would give some pointers to later paperback sales.

When the Australian distributors called me in to a promotion conference I felt that a small local success was possible; such attention had never been paid me before. The conference began impressively at a boardroom table with sales representatives from every state and a few departmental heads to lend weight. Everyone asked me questions and made notes, but it soon became plain that no-one knew how to handle the damned book and all were looking to me to design their promotion strategy. Truth was finally exposed when the Western Australian rep asked me outright did I know of any shops in Perth that sold science fiction.

There was in the end no visible promotion by the distributors. What there was—a couple of useful radio interviews—was arranged by Paul Stevens of Melbourne's Space Age Books.

The shipment of the books arrived from England a few days before the opening of Unicon IV, an important Melbourne convention with Brian Aldiss and Roger Zelazny as Guests of Honour, and to have had the books available on the site would have been useful to sales and word-of-mouth publicity. The books were not made available.

A week or so later the distributors called me in again to see a young lady who radiated confidence and efficiency and was about to launch a publicity campaign on radio, television, etc. I said *Thank you*, sure that I would hear no more of it. I heard no more of it.

There will have been administrative and commercial reasons for the backing and filling; a large company handles hundreds of titles at a time and is naturally selective about promotion, for which only tiny budgets are available. Still, it left an unpleasant feeling of having been led up the garden path and abandoned in the nettle patch.

Australian newspaper and magazine reviewers gave the book an excellent press. Most of them considered theme and intention, which the British had been vague about, allowing me the feeling that my work was at least understood in my own country.

The question of the effect of reviews on sales remains an open one. My impression is that careful behind-scenes orchestration can achieve a result. Twice during the writing of this chapter novels have been released here to favourable reviews by fairly eminent reviewers, in all major newspapers on the same day; both works featured strongly in the sales lists for the next few weeks. This type of campaign (not easily arranged, because literary editors of the magazine pages are not pleased at being manoeuvred into a free advertising stunt) is probably effective in the short term. Since the shelf life of the average novel is less than two months, the short term is important; only the very few remain in print, selling steadily for years.

These concerted efforts are rare; the probable effect of a majority of good reviews appearing in the usual fashion over a period of weeks is to interest libraries sufficiently to prevent the book sinking without trace. A string of wholly adverse reviews may undercut what little chance a new novel has in an overcrowded market, but no outrage of reviewers can undercut a pre-ordained success. Robert Heinlein's three novels before *Friday* were received with critical boredom around the world but sold like the proverbial hot cakes. The public doesn't give a damn about opinions when it has decided what it likes and, with an element of paradox, will keep on buying long after complaining that the stuff is boring and old hat.

The writer or publisher who can key into reader trends—I suspect it involves a gut response having nothing to do with surveys or statistical analysis—can laugh at opinion, and does. And good luck to him for doing intuitively what the rest of us scratch our brains over; one only wishes there was less of a lottery element in public favour. But then, the lottery element is part of what makes the game worth playing. Your next book *may* be the one, though the odds are against it.

After a while the fanzine reviews began to appear, and

most of them were unhappy with a book the professionals had led them to expect much of. They found it slow, ponderous, difficult, and few showed understanding of its themes and statements. It would have been a relief to find one honest enough to write: 'I prefer mindblowing adventure stories and this isn't one.' The cynic says that fans don't read books but only talk about them, which is unfair, but a suspicion remains that most sales are made to a silent majority that stays sensibly out of fandom's firing line, perhaps unaware of its existence. However that may be, the paperback when it appeared did reasonably well, without breaking any records.

There are no certainties to be drawn from the omens, only periods of waiting, which end sometimes with a bang or a whimper, more often with a tired pop.

I had been doodling for months with the opening chapters of a novel set in Glasgow and Edinburgh, and it had become clear that a second visit was necessary if I was to do the thing at all well. Since 1979 was Seacon year, the year of the World Science Fiction Convention in Brighton, England, the trip could also satisfy my curiosity as to what a big convention was like.

It was not particularly interesting. But then, I am not a dedicated convention-goer and rarely rise to mass enthusiasms. As usual with display-conscious determinations to please everybody, the result was soulless. It was much like the Melbourne convention of 1975, but larger, more crowded, more lavishly studded with the big names of the art; for all the relentless programming, the atmosphere was not lively; the big names appeared and disappeared in the hotel corridors and gave earnest talks in the huge auditorium (an acoustic horror of a place) where earnest audiences asked earnest questions and gave little sign of there being a life after fandom.

Editors and publishers gave large room-parties during the festivities; authors attended in droves and jostled for the attention of the hosts. There is a reason for this faintly distasteful behaviour: an indecently large proportion of science fiction is written under contract, with theme, characters, plot, length and style discussed before the writing begins; catching the ears of those with influence over contracts is a matter of urgency for all but writers successful enough or independent enough to defy the godlings. This is an American rather than an English mode, arising from the necessity to supply endless fodder to the undiscriminating while ensuring that each item will pay its way. It is surely the cause of the measles rash of series novels, propagated on the principle that if you have a success, why risk something new? Most of these production-line regurgitators are second or third string romanticists who rarely earn enough to keep themselves by writing and work like dogs for the little they get. Whether they deserve our sympathy will be taken up in the final chapter.

I was able to pick up a few British fanzine reviews of *Beloved Son*; better written and better informed than their Australian counterparts, they were no more encouraging. I had won the approval of the professional reviewers but captured no hearts among the fans at home or abroad. So I went off to Scotland to spend ten days scouring Glasgow for suitable locations, and coming to like this dour and forbidding city more than was rational.

Back in London I was taken to lunch by Charles Monteith at a club called 'L'Escargot' to be fed snails, which I found rubbery and tasteless but soused in a virulent green sauce worth eating on its own. I am a steak-and-eggs man at heart, untempted by caviare and terrified of jugged hare.

Charles told me with gentle good humour of the decline of the publishing trade, the same tale that has wound down the centuries, with this time the menacing twist of being true; the price rises that had plagued Australian importers were now striking at the production level and gloom was both the fashion and the fact. I listened with a sour taste which had nothing to do with snails, waiting to be told that under the circumstances Faber and Faber could not see their way to taking up their option on a second book; I was so sure of it that a part of my mind was making other plans. However, the matter on Charles's mind was length; he did not want another 150,000-word monster because such had become too expensive to produce. He was most Britishly delicate about it, laying his cards down gently and letting me deduce the play. I was too relieved to do other than go along with him. So this new novel, tentatively titled *Vaneglory*, would be shorter than its predecessor. Much shorter.

Carl Routledge told me the same a day or two later, in blunter terms. I returned to Australia feeling that in *Beloved Son* I had a *succès d'estime* and nothing more, and that the future held no more promise than the past. That had been the position for twenty years; only the scenery had changed.

The remaining dim possibility was a success in the States.

What happened in the US was about par for the fortunes of the book. David Hartwell, then Science Fiction Editor for Simon and Schuster's Pocket Books, bought it more or less in passing as he transferred to the job from another firm. He seemed delighted with it (remember that one takes editorial delight with a double handful of salt) but the publicity budget had already been allocated before it was added to the list, so *Beloved Son* would have to hit the market cold.

I believe that in fact it did reasonably well but not well enough to earn a reprint. *Locus*, the science fiction news magazine (called a fanzine but in fact fully professional), gave it a fairly good review, and *Algol* (a sort of semi-professional hybrid) a well-intentioned but silly one. A few others were approving, though with reservations about the Australian setting and stylistic modes with no American archetypes for easy reference. American readers can be astonishingly insular. The one real surprise came from the *Analog* reviewer, who perceived a subtle parallel with The Revelation of St John the Divine; this was a definite plus in his view, but one that has never ceased to puzzle me.

All this was satisfactory. Reviewers being what they are—a group of divergent points of view—only an unholy chorus of disapproval need trouble the writer, and that not always. Downbeat reviews are in general more useful to him, as a tradesman, than good ones. The wholly condemnatory essay that concedes no values at all can be ignored, but considered criticism backed by logic and insight is valuable even when not point accurate. The writer sees all criticism from an angle different from the critic's, and what he does about it in future books may be far from the implied recommendations of the critic, but he probably does *something* about it.

Some writers claim to pay no attention to reviews; more fools they. The author needn't bow to criticism, but he will, if his good sense is operating, think about it and select what is useful to him. A piece of fiction is not like a painting from which the artist can step back and observe it whole. The average writer is not capable of assessing his story as a complete entity, a balanced whole of interlocking words, ideas, characters, attitudes, structures and substructures, until time has allowed his perspectives to coalesce; he *needs*—always excepting the rare, great talents—informed and intelligent criticism to tell him what he has actually done, as distinct from what he set out to do.

Ideally, a typescript should lie a year or two in the drawer, to be then re-read and rehandled where necessary, but on those terms nothing would ever get into print.

Obviously no writer, if he wishes to stay sane, can take notice of every complaint against his work, but if he is an individualist with his own mode and vision, and prefers to remain so, he must not expect to be understood at once. The meanings so obvious to him are not so obvious to his readers; it requires time for an individual idiom to be absorbed into the art. If he decides that individualism does not pay and that it would be best to retire upon traditional modes, then he becomes a process worker rather than a writer—and may even make money at it.

The warning to all prospective fiction writers is: We all hope for success but only the innocent expect it. In most creative endeavour the work is the greater part of the reward.

12
Tales of
Gods and Fandom

Relaxation set in; I had not fully realized my own doubt as to whether or not I could bring off a successful raid into this foreign territory, and settling back into comparative placidity was like letting out a breath held too long.

But there is nothing placid about the science fiction community seething in fanzines and conventions, and only a yogi's calm could observe its dealings with anything like objectivity. This seems a favourable place to insert a short account of activities in the science fiction henroost, where bright birds strut their plumage while the smaller, greyer author-birds scramble for the fans' pocket money, the pecking order changes from day to day and fandom barracks at the chickenwire, urging the hens to lay and the cocks to fight.

Three or four major conventions are held each year in our capital cities and can cost the individual a daunting amount for a quick weekend in Adelaide or Sydney, with on-site accommodation at an expensive hotel, fares, meals and so on. As a result of the Guest of Honour system, whereby writers or prominent fans are invited and given the spotlight, most of Australia's writers and organizers are known throughout the country. But the parade of stars in 1975 left fandom hungry for the bigger overseas game, so the committees with better fund-raising capacities set out to bring their Guests of Honour from England and America, concentrating on those most widely known.

And a curiously mixed bag these imports have been. This is because these are not *literary* conventions: they are festivities for genre addicts, horror film buffs, comic-book lovers, fantasy painters and sculptors and the happy hordes of those seeking relief or fulfilment in an atmosphere where no confession of fixation on Weyr dragons, ET dolls or Conan the Barbarian will bring the bored or condescending smile. The fancy dress parade is a highlight of every program, featuring garb of expensive and glittering ingenuity; some attendees wear exotic regalia throughout the two or three days of the get-together.

In these mildly cockeyed surroundings—where drunkenness is a less common feature than at almost any other comparable social gathering, despite the easy availability of liquor—a few 'sercon' (fanspeak for 'serious constructive') items are introduced to placate the intellectuals and give tone to the proceedings. Sometimes these are well attended, sometimes not, and in practice the intellectual content comes down to a few harmless panel discussions of practical robotics, the probable structure of alien species or the aesthetics of the latest genre films.

These items also allow Guests of Honour (whose items are well attended) to show their paces in platform debate, hold question-and-answer sessions with the audience and be generally available to the people who want to remember that they met and talked with a favourite personality. Guests of Honour are sometimes selected on the ground of their genuine eminence in the field, but more often because they are riding a wave of popularity at the time of selection. They come in all varieties, sight unseen, and while they please their admirers by being present and touchable, few advance the cause of science fiction by as much as a bright remark. There are, of course, most honourable exceptions. Most have had Guest of Honour experience in their own countries and have learned to handle a captive audience with sufficient goodwill to smother their lack of anything useful to say. Most of them, when you can get them alone with the fan-group persona laid aside, appear as hard-working professionals with families to keep, pleasant enough to talk to and rather like most of the commonplace people you know. If some of the more successful tend to believe their own publicity build-up, that is a human failing not confined to science fiction writers.

Early in 1977 a three-week workshop was promoted, on a larger scale than the first and located in the functionally ideal surroundings of Monash University, with a different professional writer overseeing each week. The three professionals came from like but divergent literary cultures, to highlight differences of approach. Vonda McIntyre from the USA supervised the first week and Chris Priest from England the last, with myself in the middle. At that time I had published no science fiction, but the administrators recognized that fundamentals do not vary, that story-writing remains story-writing, in or out of genre.

My insistence on an Australian approach to writing (meaning only that writers ignore overseas models and do their own thinking) was known but misunderstood. What, they asked, did I mean by an 'Australian idiom'? Stories featuring gum-trees, wombats, Ayers Rock, sunburnt heroes and grim outback heroines who said 'dinkum' and 'cobber' every second line? Such narrowness did not impress them. Their lack of imagination did not impress me.

That mystical 'sense of wonder', hailed by enthusiasts but rarely achieved in a cliché-ridden genre, seemed basic to their ambitions, so a certain unease was evident when both Vonda and Chris told them to develop their natural approaches and not look to American or English models. It became more evident when, in the second week, I set out deliberately to degrade the sense-of-wonder ideal by setting creative exercises that forced attention on everyday surroundings (such as one's own back yard for a setting) and on those realities of the everyday which underpin any fiction, however fantastic. They rose, not too willingly but at least gamely, to the hurdles of realism and some of the best work was done within those unpromising parameters.

Between the three of us we made a useful impression,

shown in the collection *The View from the Edge* (Nor-strilia Press, 1977) that I later compiled from stories written at the workshop.

Having other projects moving at the time, I was unable to see much of Vonda or Chris, but I sat in on Vonda's final session in the interest of making a smooth transition from her method to mine, and found that her technique was almost identical with that of Ursula Le Guin, though neither she nor any of us could reproduce the Le Guin magic. It was no trouble to follow on from her, with little change of emphasis at first.

Vonda knew what she was about in the workshop but I found her difficult to talk to outside. She had, I think, a natural reserve accentuated by a fierce feminism that was then making explosions in American science fiction, and was still in the militant stage where women were be-leaguered and men the enemy. But the workshoppers liked her and she laid a faultless ground for my middle week to build on.

Chris had operated at workshops in England and coasted through it; he was very popular with the young writers and displayed an effervescence I had not seen in him in London.

The running of a live-in workshop is formidably expen-sive, particularly as we carried the creative process through to the editing and publishing stages, as the Le Guin work-shop had also. The justification for the existence of such an ant-nest of energy is that it is far more intensive in its demands on the writers than is possible in any classroom course in Short Story Writing or Literary Appreciation and more deeply searching into the capacities of the young writers.*

* The method consists, basically, of having every submitted story read by every member of the workshop, then assessed and criticized in open session. The task of the professional monitor or leader or overseer—no definitive word has been settled on but 'teacher', with its didactic connotations, is not applicable—is to steer discussion away from trivialities and towards crucial factors, as well as to inculcate the tenets of fair and proper criticism as distinct from simple statements of like and dislike. The workshop could be de-scribed as a course in literary criticism, which the writers are en-couraged to apply to their own product. Once they have caught on

The Literature Board of the Australia Council supplied a proportion of the funds for the Monash project, and the importation of McIntyre and Priest was justified by the results; they did what was asked of them with the dedication that takes no account of a sixteen-hour day. That they and I enjoyed it was a personal bonus. An intensive workshop can be grindingly hard on everyone concerned, but in a successful one the sense of achievement pays for everything.

I have argued since that our local writers, such as Lee Harding and Damien Broderick, can handle these courses as efficiently as any overseas writer (the method is gruelling but not intrinsically difficult), but in 1977 they were little known to the prospective workshop attendees and a bait was needed to attract their confidence.

The bait was expensive and without the Literature Board contribution might have been unreachable, but I believe that on this occasion it paid dividends in the fostering of talent. There has been a more progressive spirit in Australian science fiction ever since.

In 1978 the Melbourne University Science Fiction Association staged a convention, Unicon IV, and broke precedent by inviting *two* topline overseas writers as co-Guests of Honour, an arrangement that reportedly overjoyed neither of the egos involved when they heard of it. But they shared top billing in decorous amity.

It was a convention whereat things went inexorably wrong, mainly because of the inexperience of the committee in handling tightly structured programs. Necessary people were for ever unfindable, program items were shuffled with little thought for the performers, and some items vanished without trace; a decent veil must be drawn over the events that made black comedy of the presentation of some local awards. It was fandom at its engaging zaniest, plugging holes as fast as they appeared while watching fearfully for fresh cracks in the dike.

---

to what constitutes useful criticism they tend to welcome peer assessment. Since new work is produced throughout the course the changes in personal approach, sometimes radical, are readily observed.

Later committees learned from that one, and now in each state a body of fans exists who know just how to run a convention from scratch. The rest of us sit back and let them do it, and afterwards complain bitterly of faults visible only to nitpickers. As ever, the willing donkey is flogged for his pains.

The American guest that year was Roger Zelazny, a writer very popular with fans but less so with the literati, who saw him as a well of unfulfilled promise. Early in his career he had produced some excellent novellas and one novel with some claim to neo-classic status (in so far as the term can be applied to work less than twenty years old, meaning 'regarded as outstanding in the genre'), but by the time he came to Australia he was writing what I think of as pseudo-fantasies, pointless adventures in bizarre settings.

Still, the writer of *The Dream Master* and 'A Rose for Ecclesiastes' was no nonentity. He emerged as a tallish, slender man who confided unexpectedly that his sport is fencing. As a platform performer he did quietly what was required of him, astonishing me only when he outlined a system of literary characterization (claiming to have been taught it in a university) wherein humanity was reduced to three basic types, which seemed to be gods, kings and commoners. Or perhaps shock caused me to hear it incorrectly. I could only conclude, with some foreboding for the future of science fiction, that they do things differently in America.

The committee shopping for an overseas guest usually has only a wishful idea of what it will get; it learns the hard way that the pyrotechnics of the novelist rarely illumine his fleshly presence, while those hoping for literary enlightenment may end in teeth-grinding dismay.

Zelazny was not a pushful performer and could not shine against the bravura of Brian Aldiss. Aldiss the convention personality is as smooth, witty and effortless as his prose. He has, as they say, star quality, which he projects with genial authority. We met for a few minutes when he arrived in Melbourne and exchanged meaningless phrases. I would have liked to make good some of the unsatisfactoriness of the English encounter but felt, when it

172

came to the point, that we had nothing to say to each other. In our work and attitudes we are poles apart.

His co-Guest of Honour speech got off to an irritating start with a spatter of Australian jokes, including a Rolf Harris old-timer that, spoken by an Englishman, sounded unfortunately like an effort to drop to colonial level. These were only a loosening-up exercise (every vaudevillian knows that once you crack the first laugh they're yours) and charm came to the fore in the body of the speech, an entertaining ramble through personal experiences. The following year, at the World Convention in England, I heard him give much the same speech (with English jokes), still sounding as impromptu as ever but shaped, honed and polished to perfection. Aldiss is fully professional with an audience, and professionalism means hoarding resources and refurbishing them; his speech was a lesson in doing a thing well, and then doing it better.*

Ad-libbing experiences at Unicon IV were less fortunate. One afternoon I gave a talk on some subject now forgotten and was probably laying into the shortcomings of genre science fiction (then my habit on every public occasion, playing the gadfly) when I spotted Aldiss at the back of the hall, watching me and plainly displeased. Displeased he surely was. Half an hour later we were on the platform together as members of a discussion panel and he snapped up one of my remarks with an openly condescending reference to some master works with which, he felt, I was plainly unfamiliar. It happened that I was fully familiar, and replied that after fifty years of reading science fiction I knew the major texts as well as he did and didn't share his reverence for some of them.

I think the incipient juvenility of this exchange hit both of us; we let the matter drop dead. The couple of hundred fans in the hall would have loved a spit-and-snarl session

* The climax of Aldiss's Australian speech, repeated at the English Seacon, later appeared, with embellishments, as a short story, 'Foreign Bodies', in an Aldiss collection under that title, published in Singapore in 1981. Spoken or written, it is a good story, a wry little commentary on the tricksiness of memory. It is set in Sumatra and I, unrepentant, at once think again of Somerset Maugham.

between experts but we both knew better than to provide it. We met only once more during his visit, as opposites at dinner, and were unadventurously polite. We are fated to remain acquaintances at arm's length.

While in Australia Aldiss addressed audiences of students and academics at universities in both Sydney and Adelaide, and science fiction could scarcely have found a more persuasive apostle. He justified the expense of bringing him here, which cannot be said of many who followed.

Terry Carr was another who justified his fare. In 1979 another workshop was held in Sydney. It was less successful than the earlier two; the standard of entry stories was lower, the venue had no air-conditioning and the midsummer sun was relentless. Rousing enthusiasm in attendees and myself was a daily chore, but at least one success story emerged in Leanne Frahm, who has been selling her fiction ever since.

I was glad to hand over at the end of a week to Terry Carr, who had been flown in from the USA. He had been an inspiration on the part of Petrina Smith, arranger of the workshop; he was and is the best of the regular American anthologists, of whom there seem to be dozens, and his experience of the field made him a natural choice. Having published a volume of his own short stories, including at least one really superior tale, 'The Dance of the Changer and the Three', he knew the needs from both sides of the editorial desk.

Lee Harding had then just published his fine anthology *Rooms of Paradise*, containing a novella of mine, and in the process of breaking the conversational ice—never easy for me—I presented Terry with a copy. Without looking at it he said 'I would like you to write something for my annual *Universe* series.' Since I had published no other short work, this had to mean that he had read and approved of *Beloved Son*. I suppose I mumbled the usual appreciation and he went off to rest from his Pacific crossing.

In the morning he said one of those things that leave you treading mental water: 'I read your story last night and I would still like you to write something for me.'

Read that how you will, but he published that tale, 'In a

Petri Dish Upstairs', in his *Best Science Fiction of the Year* 9, so at least it had not been a put-down. And of course I wrote a story for *Universe*; who wouldn't, after that?

We saw little more of each other because I had to hand over and get back to Melbourne, but we met later in the year at the Brighton convention, when, sitting in a beach-front café, he announced out of the blue: 'You speak just as you write, all Germanic roots and very few Latinisms.'

This mildly paralysing bit of café society chitchat was not unlike being told that you have a bricklayer's hands when you have always secretly admired their slender grace. Wondering whether Germanic roots were or were not sinful, I muttered mock-cheerfully that I would never write another word without checking its etymology. Terry replied sternly: 'You get told that sort of thing at conventions.'

The penny dropped at last; from the moment of that Sydney meeting I had been dealing with a deadpan humorist. Life with Terry Carr could be bewildering but stimulating. I don't know how he handled those Sydney workshoppers but he screwed some much improved writing out of them.

While the more self-consciously literate Australian fans tend to regard British science fiction writers as 'better' (amorphous word) on the whole than their American counterparts, the preference of the general reader is shown by the guests invited for the conventions. With the single exception of Brian Aldiss they have been American to a man—to a man indeed, with not another woman since Ursula Le Guin. Have they never heard of such intelligent *and* popular writers as Alice Sheldon ('James Tiptree Jr'), Joanna Russ and Kate Wilhelm? Or such Britons as Ian Watson, Keith Roberts and James White? Of course they have, but the emphasis is on popularity to please the mass audience, with a consequent leaning towards undemanding, middle-of-the-road competence. Meaning, bluntly, mediocrity.

The results are usually dull, occasionally unpredictable.

In 1980 Gordon Dickson arrived, another unassuming,

pleasant man who might be anybody's neighbour. He is professionally prolific, with a number of awards for his stories, stylistically indistinguishable from a score of his peers, one of those necessary, dependable folk who hold the strong middle ground of the genre. He has been for many years writing a twelve-volume *magnum opus*—with breaks for potboilers—about a universe fragmented into incompatible cultural philosophies. There seems, in the couple I have read, to be an emphasis on military philosophy as a binding force, and my impression is that Dickson's view of soldiering and soldier psychology is romantically simplistic. I took the opportunity to ask him (cautiously) about it and was only confused by his explanation that empathy lies at the heart of it all and that empathy is a comparatively modern concept. It is certainly a modern word, but for the good of international relations I resisted the temptation to ask had he never heard of Jesus, Gautama, the Chinese philosophers . . .

Later in the year came Joe Haldeman and his wife, Gay. Haldeman also writes mainly about soldiering, with some authority springing from his Vietnam experience. His novel *The Forever War* projected the changing conditions of war into a receding future, won a Hugo award and was more interesting than most of its kind, yet did not seem to encompass any real understanding of the military mind or to reach the human being inside the soldier. Yet, after his return to America, he sent me a copy of his first, non-science-fiction novel, *A War Year*, an unambitious demonstration that he can write accurately and well about real soldiers. It seems to me far better work than he has published since, a minor but notable contribution to the documenting of that spectacularly sickening war.

Is there, in science fiction, an intrinsic dampener that kills the truth of some human projections? Frederik Pohl, Gardner Dozois and others with service backgrounds have written military characterizations of such freezing unreality, despite touches of neo-pornography, as to make one wonder whether they did their service blindfold. It is noticeable that Brian Aldiss, who has mined his wartime experience for a couple of nostalgic and realistic army comedies, rarely introduces service characters into his science fiction, as though he senses that the artificial environment will not accommodate their essential humanity. War is one of science fiction's major preoccupations and one about which it displays an ignorance hard to credit in a world whose entire population is sooner or later brushed by it.

At the risk of overworking the adjective, Joe Haldeman was unassuming to the edge of self-apology, referring often to 'the level on which he worked' as though conscious of operating in a second-class milieu. Perhaps, but we could do with a few more to speak as straightforwardly and unglorifyingly about their way of earning a living.

The Haldemans, husband and wife, said and did nothing memorable on their visit but left behind them something rare in the frenzy of literary lionizing, a sense of charm having nothing to do with showbiz.

In 1981 a Melbourne group of fantasy-film enthusiasts organized a smallish convention, Cinecon, which lost them a lot of money but was attended by professional and amateur film-makers with ideas to communicate. Bringing Robert Bloch from Hollywood in a bid for popular attention turned out to be one they couldn't afford but which under better circumstances would have given some cachet to a brave attempt.

Bloch is a screen writer best known as the author of *Psycho*, the novel from which Hitchcock made one of his most macabre films, but is also the author of some neat and pointed science fiction from earlier days. Asked to meet him, I was confronted at a small dinner party by a most unmacabre man of about my own age who apparently remembered my critical essays because he said with a straight face: 'I am surprised to meet you; I have always thought you were a pseudonym.'

Another in the Terry Carr mould. Almost I found myself apologizing for the fact of flesh.

Bloch was another no-nonsense professional—always more interesting than those who feel it incumbent on them to behave as 'serious artists'—who loved early cinema. We

177

were able to swap reminiscences of famous antiquities, memories of *The Perils of Pauline* and *The Clutching Hand*, the original Saturday afternoon excitements of *The Lost World*, *Metropolis* and the Lon Chaney horror feasts— two ageing men envying the two small boys who could no longer respond with the total awe and wonder of innocence.

Bloch was a comfortable man to be with; you didn't have to fear that at any moment he would talk about his writing, with that sudden defensive caution that means he knows it isn't as good as you are expected to pretend. I don't know what his visit may have done for local film-making; probably little, for he said nothing to set our minds ablaze; I like to remember him as one more node of good sense in the playground of fantasy.

No fan organization brought Anne McCaffrey to Australia; she passed through on a publicity tour organized by her publishers, but the Perth fans gathered her in for a small convention whereat fandom enjoyed her ecstatically. There I watched the performance of a theatre-trained personality whose manipulation never quite hid the glint of self-mockery.

Anne McCaffrey lives in Ireland, breeds horses, has some theatrical past and is currently a heroine of world fandom by reason of half a dozen novels in which humans and dragons co-exist in useful amity. From her first appearance it was plain that here was an old trouper who knew how to grab an audience and tie it in knots of her choosing. The fans wanted to know about dragons, so she told them about dragons and impressed on them in passing the correct attitude towards her books; they adopted the correct attitude. The fairy godmother took over without any fancy wand-waving, subjecting the audience with the simple assumption that they were her slaves. They were.

When one, greatly daring, asked were her fire-breathing dragons 'scientific' or only fantastical, she stood firmly for science, explaining that they carried in their throats a chemical deposit that ignited spontaneously with oxygen. There are several agents available for that effect but I wondered (in silence) did they also have throats lined with a heat-resistant natural ceramic? I knew better than to ask; she would only have fixed me with a sardonic smile and replied 'Sure; how else?'

Only once did her self-possession falter briefly. At one of her book-signing sessions a teenager arrived almost staggering under a double armload of McCaffrey paperbacks, scarcely able to see over them. They would have been the collected hoard of his local group—old, stained, dog-eared, loved to death—wished on him to obtain signatures for all who could not attend. She hesitated fractionally in disbelief as the stuff slid and toppled on the table, then set grimly to signing her way through treasures that said more than rave reviews. The price of idolatry can be disconcerting.

Later she came to Melbourne, where Mervyn Binns, the proprietor of Space Age Books, hosted one of his Chinese-food dinner parties for her. The dinner guest was a different Anne, free of the necessities of staying in character, letting her hair a little way down to talk about horses and Ireland as well as some undecorated shop about the realities of contract hassles and the difficulty of doing the things you want to after a resounding success in one narrow line. I asked a few questions about the razzle-dazzle side of mass-produced science fiction, and she was fairly forthcoming without actually dishing the dirt on anyone. She was more interested, and thoroughly approving, when I suggested that more than a few big names were really dressed in the emperor's new clothes. At the end of the evening she planted a quite unexpected goodnight kiss on my cheek, with a smile that said—I think—'We know it's just a game.'

Anne McCaffrey was a lesson in playing the glittering symbol without for a moment becoming lost in the part. A different sort of method acting, from one who knew what she owed to her audience, and paid it.

1982 produced a bumper crop of Very Important People, with results hilarious and/or thought-provoking.

First came Larry Niven, a science fiction phenomenon

179

in the Silverberg Golden Boy class, a writer of 'hard science' stories—that is, tales based for the most part on accurate science and strict extrapolation or speculation—that have been popular because of their liveliness, a feature not common among 'hard science' novelists. I met him at a party in South Yarra, one of those meet-your-hero squeezes where youthful fans covered every inch of floor space and we few ageing squares stepped gingerly over bodies, in search of standing room.

Niven occupied mid-floor, nursing a drink and saying little. Another reserved, quiet type, I decided, until he opened his mouth and dropped a few pearls that belong in everybody's treasury of the dreadful.

He had recently collaborated with Jerry Pournelle in a sort of mini-blockbuster called *Lucifer's Hammer*. It was, he said, a novel that challenged the mainstream on its own terms. He meant literary values, whatever those may be in any given context. This could be excused in a proud father displaying his genetically superior child, but in fact the book was one of the currently popular disaster novels wherein a massive body from space threatened to crash into the Earth, a presentable representative of its kind and full of interesting data on the probable results of such a collision. The literary values were less evident; neither writer actually mangled the English language, but neither did they use it other than as a tool for unvarnished statement while showing no sign of having ever observed a human being as anything more than a narrative convenience.

Anyone may be allowed the odd regrettable remark but a reputation may hang on not exceeding the quota. Niven proceeded to praise James Clavell's historical romance *Shogun* as science fiction on the ground that it deals with a clash of cultures. This was only the minor sin of stretching definition too far; what followed was otherwise. *Shogun*, he announced, establishing his critical rating once and for all, is a better novel than *War and Peace*.

John Bangsund and I left soon after. The staunchest politeness could not stifle laughter indefinitely.

It is unlikely that Niven did any damage to the young

minds present; the young, despite their flamboyant loyalties, are not all that damned gullible.

Frank Herbert, Guest of Honour at an Adelaide convention, was very different. He shares with Heinlein the distinction of being one of the two most popular science fiction writers of all time; his *Dune* novels have broken the boundaries of science fiction readership, selling in millions.

He is a pleasantly spoken, affable man with a ready humour and an appreciation of the neat point neatly made, approachable among the fans but never adopting the 'one of the boys' attitude, which is so easily punctured. His Guest of Honour speech was the best since the Aldiss visit, witty and full of pertinent comment; afterwards, reading the Adelaide *Advertiser*, I found he had given the key points, in almost identical terms, to the press on the day before. Well, why not? Like Aldiss, he is kept in demand by his enormous reputation and so has developed a repertoire of gambits for public use. It is a common-sense attitude; the problem of being original and yet consistent in cross-country performances could be formidable.

I sat with Herbert in the audience through several of the convention items, and by sitting a little apart we were able to hold our own *sotto voce* discussion of the topics. He is as ready-witted and perceptive as his prepared speeches would have you believe, the ideal convention guest, amusing, affable and intelligent. It cannot be said that his presence added anything to the progress of science fiction, which requires more than pleasantries to tickle its self-satisfaction, but at least he left with a good name and no trail of dropped clangers.

A week later the Fellowship of Australian Writers put on a small dinner party in Melbourne for Herbert; I was invited but declined, giving a specious reason. I found it impossible to explain that in the freer atmosphere of a small party conversation would inevitably turn to the Herbert *oeuvre*, a subject I had avoided in Adelaide, and that I would not perjure myself by joining in praise, or even by remaining silent during the mass approvals of books whose writer I liked very well as a human being but cannot stomach as a novelist. Sadly, I find his *Dune* books

181

and most of his others pretentious, loaded with paraphrases of other people's aphorisms and presented with a labyrinthine cunning whose promised revelations never appear.

Yet he is one of the writers I have most enjoyed meeting, and I am old-fashioned enough to believe that the time and place for critical loggerheads is not at a party where the one under fire is the principal guest.

The visit of Jack Vance as Guest of Honour of the major Melbourne convention of 1982 threw a curious light on fan partisanship and in-group literary criticism. Vance is a minor hero of the genre. He has written for nearly forty years in a variety of modes, from 'hard science' ('The Gift of Gab') to a sort of fairy-tale picaresque exemplified by the adventures of a rogue protagonist in *The Eyes of the Overworld*, but with little change of style from one type of tale to another. His enchanted followers, as beguiled as Malcolm Edwards in *The Encyclopedia of Science Fiction*, will speak of his style 'tending towards the baroque', his 'unusual vocabulary' and 'detached and ironic narrative voice', yet a series of cuts through any of his works will rarely yield a page of better than commonplace expression of simple states and reactions. His special flair is for the devising of imaginary cultures, always ingenious, colourful and romantic, and devised specifically to be ingenious, colourful and romantic; they rarely have any foundation in sociological or political likelihood and offer little to a reader demanding intellectual stimulus. His novels are true 'fantastic romances', with little pretence at being more.

Yet something in his work, some quality (possibly of simple strangeness?) that eludes my enjoyment of his ingenuities, causes his devotees—a *mot juste*—to hail him as a master of language, a prince of sociological subtleties, a stylist magnetic and superb. Many of his books are published in handsome, large-format, expensively illustrated editions and one can only conclude that these extravagances pay their way or they would not exist.

This is not to suggest that Vance is a nonentity. His imaginative virtue is great though his plotting facility is mundane; he is always good for a refreshing chuckle where more portentous writers become portentous bores. He is entertaining and original where too many of his fellows are plodders in outworn tracks, but these genialities do not qualify him as a literary master.

The thought of a Jack Vance imprisoned and deluded by his fan image was daunting, but the real man was as quietly reserved as Joe Haldeman and as accurate in self-appraisal as Le Guin or Bloch. Somewhere near my own age and relaxing into that comfort which pays only the necessary lip service to dress and presence, Vance could easily be the proprietor of a country store, leaning on the counter in shirt sleeves to discuss the price of fat lambs. His speech was careful, phrased to avoid misinterpretation. I felt that this was part of an uncomfortable awareness of his technicoloured image in fandom. Events showed that he had reason.

One of the convention items was a panel of Vance 'experts' questioning the man on his work. This type of item has become almost *de rigueur* and is designed, presumably, to allow the panellists to elicit literary and psychological undertones from a writer speaking about his productions. In fact this rarely happens and the reason is only partly inexperience in this type of questioning. The panel is always composed of fans biased in the writer's favour (inevitably, since they are the ones most familiar with his output) and the questions tend to be thinly disguised compliments on the lines of 'Where do you get those fabulous ideas?'

It is recorded that Vonda McIntyre, on being actually asked that idiot question, replied 'Schenectady'. An Australian counterpart might try Upotipotpon.

The panel questioning Vance made a fairly knowledgeable and intelligent crew. Sadly they were, all four, worshippers at the shrine, more intent on displaying their detailed familiarity with Vance's fiction than on mining useful information. The unfortunate Vance became quickly aware of the problem and tried to handle it with genial, commonsense answers, which did not succeed in stemming the flattery of the questions. A query was soon raised that threatened to break the patient camel's back. Didn't Mr

Vance feel that in the final novel of the *Star Kings* series, hero and villain finally exchanged their philosophic roles, thus bringing the hero . . . Vance replied with some emphasis that he felt nothing of the sort, making it plain that no literary subtlety was in question.

Recognizing no snub, the questioner ploughed on in a fashion that embarrassed me for Vance as plainly as it embarrassed him. It was not the new question that irritated so much as the preamble, stating in so many words that Vance's prose was the aesthetic equal of the best being produced today.

Vance answered flatly that he considers himself a plain and straightforward writer. That this is an accurate description of his style, given by a man who knows just what he is about, cut no ice with the panel. They wanted a hero and would have one. At last came the inevitable question about future plans, and Vance reeled off a string of ideas—perhaps a new novel in this series or some short stories in that, or maybe a fresh idea he had been revolving . . .

Yes, but which one would he write first?

Said Vance, 'Whichever I get a contract for.'

The businesslike commercialism—thoroughly justified commercialism, I think—of this answer, with all its implications for the flowery offerings of the panel, seemed to pass unnoticed; the love feast went on. What manner of worship is it when the god himself is unable to crack the iron devotion of his acolytes?

It is only right to applaud Jack Vance as a tradesman with a proper appreciation of his market value and no delusion of grandeur. He is just the nice chap to engage in 'matters of discussion proper to writers: money, sex and beer'. It was a shame that his fans could not see him so. And a little disturbing.

No arrangement of these snippets would properly portray the ferment of fandom or the network communication of science fiction writers, most of whom are acquainted with each other in a fashion unmatched in other genres or even in such literary organizations as the PEN Club. It cannot be too strongly emphasized that fandom exists for amusement and socializing; its interest in literature is a sop to the few who demand this cloak over the fancy dress—the same few whose deeper interest leaves them responsible for the administration and programming of fannish events. Similarly the writers, many of whom are in fact interested in literature, are sufficiently amused to enter into the spirit of the thing; some plainly find it an effort but only a few publicly flout the demands of fandom; most go through the motions with good grace and some possibly find the publicity useful.

Now, all this is reasonable while it is accepted that conventions are not literary occasions but festivities. It may seem less reasonable when it is recalled that requests for Literature Board funding have been made by convention committees, on heaven knows what literary grounds, and that some Guests of Honour might not have been brought here had the money not been granted. Trans-oceanic flights are not cheap. I have pointed out that some of these grants have been justified by results and that the guests have been prepared cheerfully to work their passage by operating workshops and engaging in some public speaking, but the decline in standards since the visit of Brian Aldiss has been dismaying. Le Guin, McIntyre, Priest, Aldiss (whose visit was not funded) and Carr were good value for readers, young writers and in some cases academics; too many others were nice people with little to offer but their signatures on the paperback volumes of their fans, and any random substitutes would have served as well. Not all of these later visits were funded; one must hope that few of them were.

Convention committees have not been overly concerned with bringing in people who could give value for money spent. (Or have they merely confused popularity with literary merit?) We have seen few of the writers who could stimulate not only science fiction but the local literary scene in general, the people with strong ideas and a strong expression of them. We could have asked Joanna Russ, Thomas M. Disch, Ian Watson, Gene Wolfe,* Keith Roberts, Hilary Bailey, Franz Rottensteiner and others representing

* While I was writing this, Gene Wolfe was in fact being asked. He is to be Guest of Honour at the World Convention in Melbourne in 1985.

intellectual areas as yet barely touched on in Australia. Ballard and Moorcock are probably unobtainable, being two who usually refuse to face fandom in the raw, and it may be merely wishful to dream of reaching into Russia for the Strugatski brothers (yet why shouldn't the attempt be made?), but there are many others who could jolt the aficionados, as well as the younger writers and some of our abysmal reviewers, into the modern era. Too much of what we receive here is filtered, misreported, garbled, secondhand and dated.

Fandom, then, is for all its noise and scurry a negligible influence on quality, and it is numerically small in proportion to the number of readers of science fiction. It is doubtful that all the world's fans—that is, those who belong to fan clubs, publish fanzines and attend conventions—could create a best seller by buying one copy each of a single title.

So who reads the millions of copies of the *Dune* novels or rushes to buy the new Heinlein or Asimov? Who are the public the authors actually write for?

A silent multitude forms the readership that keeps science fiction alive in the market, a multitude with no desire to cavort in fancy dress under the eye of a Guest of Honour, engage in polemic about telepathic aardvarks on Capella 10 or compile a periodical gossip sheet (fanzine) in order to feel partnership in a social bloc. It reads for the solitary pleasure of reading, which is a part of man's communing with himself, needing no bolstering by others with similar tastes, content to receive as the author intended, form his own opinions and make no further fuss about it. It contains academics and labourers, nurses and politicians, professional men and waitresses, actresses and clerks. I can vouch for several in these categories and a hundred others, but would get no thanks for naming names while the image of the lurid cover and the bug-eyed monster still hangs over the genre.

Not even if they read the respectable authors? Like Aldiss, Watson, Le Guin, Lem, the Strugatskis, Ballard? The trouble here is that for the most part they don't read those authors; they read for relaxation rather than for instruction or elevation, and at the end of the working day a rampaging monster is more fun than Watsonian metaphysics, Ballardian metaphor or convoluted Strugatskian satire.

The more important writers, meaning those with something to say and some style with which to say it, are the quarry of the intellectual reader whose conception of relaxation embraces the easy absorption of an ingenious idea, a stimulating argument, an effective use of structure, a thoughtfully presented paradigm. These writers do not sell to a mass readership. They don't sell much at all outside of a small but interested public. Quality, as ever, is left at the bottom of the barrel. The Priests and Watsons and Ballards have a thin time of it financially (that is not metaphor but hard fact) although they are some of the people who give to science fiction most of what makes it worth while. Their innovation of today becomes the hack writer's commonplace—stripped of meaning—tomorrow. Everybody knows their names and knows they are 'good' but everybody *buys* dependable Heinlein or Herbert or Asimov who will neither puzzle nor discomfort.

Occasionally one or other will make a killing and prosper for a year or two, but as a rule he/she will continue to work for less than a labourer's wage because the work counts more than the wage. Through the years I have heard of many in straitened circumstances, on relief or even forced to sell their homes, but I have heard of only one arrogant and foolish enough to berate the world for not preserving science fiction writers in honoured comfort.*

So what is the relationship between fans and writers?

* In 1982 Barry Malzberg, an American science fiction writer, published a collection of essays, *Engines of the Night*, a revealing behind-the-scenes view of American writing and publishing in the mass market area. Its general excellence was, however, marred by alarming overstatements of the literary achievements of some very ordinary genre writers and distorted by a fictional climax in which a figure representing the American Science Fiction Writer makes a convention speech affirming his dedication to his 'art': 'We tried desperately to say something because we were the only ones who could, and however halting our language, tuneless the song, it was ours.' Having thus hymned what was in fact decades of mediocrity, the speaker bursts into tears, presumably for the hard-headed world that resolutely denies worship to the mediocre. One recalls Oscar Wilde's remark about *The Old Curiosity Shop*, to the effect that only a man with a heart of stone could read the death of Little Nell without bursting into tears—of laughter.

For those with strong individual followings (there are competent writers of romantic science fiction adventure, like Jacqueline Lichtenberg and Marion Zimmer Bradley, who have their own fan clubs) the relationship is one of continual feedback, allowing the writer to know what is wanted and assuring the readers that that is what they will get.

For the less fortunate, on the lowest rung of publication, appearing only in paperback and lucky to sell out the print run, there is little public relationship of any kind. Many of these are fans who have graduated to the big time only to discover how small it is. For practical purposes they remain fans.

And the big names? The men and women whose names in the advance publicity mean convention crowds in eager hush? (But not necessarily sales of books.) Some, I think, genuinely enjoy performing; some grab at the chance of a paid holiday while guest-of-honouring a convention; others feel appearance incumbent upon them, that a refusal might offend.

The final truth appears when these eagles gather at a World Convention. Each makes his/her obligatory platform appearance in a program designed to display them all. And then he or she mingles with the fans? Don't believe it. Editors, writers and critics flock together in private parties, talking the real shop that few fans get to hear, while the fans wander the hotel corridors or hold parties of their own or watch ancient sci-fi (as distinct from science fiction) films they have seen a dozen times before. The professionals don't gather to talk to fans but to each other. Sensibly so; that way they keep in touch with what is going on in their world of publishing upheavals, editorial restrictions and shattered hopes.

In Australia, where many science fiction writers have graduated from fandom, we are as well known to the locals as the boy next door and as little respected, which makes pretence as unnecessary as it would be silly. That we should be spinners of the stuff of dreams is not seen as remarkable, only useful; after all, they knew us before we began spinning, and publication has changed nothing.

Perhaps we local writers have the best of it in reader relationship; nobody is over respectful or pretentiously literary with us as they too often tend to be with visitors, so the exchange of views is at least downright. This is healthy for both reader and writer. I am reminded of Ursula Le Guin telling us that her three children were not overly impressed with her success in science fiction, or with science fiction itself. It was just 'something Mom does'.

Just another kind of writing.

And so it is.

There is no need for anyone to cry for the poor science fiction writers, least of all themselves. They know what they are doing and that they are doing it because they wish to, aware that the rewards are small. Save in the cases of the very few the rewards of literature have always been small. There is every reason to try to increase them but none to weep over non-recognition in a world with troubles of its own.

13

How to Spoil
a Promising Career

After *Beloved Son* my work became more than ever before complicated by personal obstinacy as well as by the evolution of the science fiction scene. This chapter is about the consequences of doing what you want to do instead of listening to advisers who know what the market will do to your wilfulness. They were right. Aspiring writers will observe the pitfalls and how to avoid them, usually at the price of their creative souls.

One Glasgow day in 1976 I strolled along the north embankment of the Clyde, using the pale June sunshine to snap a few pictures. My Polaroid was not today's compact instrument but something twice the size and awkwardly shaped, hanging by a strap and banging a bruise on my left buttock as I walked, and a girl sitting on one of the promenade benches said 'Good heavens, a tourist! In Glasgow!'

Her Highland accent, not as rough as the Glaswegian burr, which can be almost incomprehensible, had enough lilt in it to make an amused but friendly comment of what could have been a contemptuous throwaway. When I stopped she went on, 'I thought they kept you all cooped up in the ferry boats on Loch Lomond.' That she made all this acceptable, even intriguing, was a fine turn of personality, because every tourist learns quickly that the Britons wish nothing better than to see the back of him, after he has handed over his cash. I have to play fair and admit that not all the Britons are like that, but an impression of grasping rudeness can be dismaying at first; they are in fact much like anybody else, Australians included, in

191

that you must sound out the proper level of approach, but the Britons won't go out of their way to help you find it. You will meet more amiability in Scotland, but should not build up unreasonable expectations there either.

The girl asked what brought me to Glasgow and when I explained that I had a friend in Australia who had been born there she said 'Give the lucky man my love,' meaning that he had escaped the ruinous city while she could not.

By the end of the afternoon I had the encounter and the character that, dramatized and shifted to another part of the city, were to become the plot germ of *Vaneglory*. I think she would have been highly entertained by the rapacious huntress into which she became transformed by the requirement of fiction.

An ex-soldier whom I met in the bar of the Rob Roy, a pub in an inner suburb, told me improbable tales for as long as I cared to pour whisky (which he couldn't have afforded for himself) down his neck and became the physical model for 'Donald' in the novel, but resembled him in nothing else.

I returned to Australia with two characters building in my mind and two cities to write about, but no theme or story, though it had occurred to me that an abandoned shipyard on the Clyde would be a reasonable place to lay the long, narrow hull of such a starship as I had imagined for *Beloved Son*, since it would not need to be erected vertically. (This became only a background item in the story, but I have discovered that airship frames were in fact built in British shipyards in the 1930s and with the present revival of interest in them may be again.) Also, I had been thinking desultorily about the social and psychological consequences of an extended human life span—say, several thousand years. Eternal life, one of the most ancient dreams of a desirable human condition, seemed, the more I thought about it, an unmitigated disaster. The parts were there, rattling around, waiting on time to settle them.

I had not intended an actual sequel to *Beloved Son* but its milieu was ideal for my new purpose. In the end I lifted four characters over into *Vaneglory*, giving some psychological continuity, and shifted the action forward a couple of years.

With only a few chapters in experimental longhand draft,

I mentioned casually to John Foyster that I proposed to use a fair amount of Scottish dialogue, and he surprised and shocked me a little by saying firmly that he found 'dialect' in fiction irritating. Many people say they 'just can't stand' this or that technique, but I had thought of them as superficial readers interested only in the surface of the text and unwilling to bring anything to it, on a par with those who 'can't bear' first person narrative but lap it up without noticing if the story takes their fancy. Coming from John, whose appreciation of forbiddingly difficult texts commands my respect, this set me back a mental pace or two; 'dialect' could turn out a serious barrier to acceptance.

No matter, and in any case too late. The private internal magic was working and there could be no turning back. Defiantly I added another Scottish-speaking character to the cast, basing the physical description on a friend, Jim Dunwoodie, the ex-Glasgow man whose talk of Scotland had sent me there in the first place. Hanging the physical aspects of real people on characters (but providing them with wholly fictional personalities) helps visualization of complex activities and scenes.

The writing went easily, too easily. I found myself with fifty thousand useless words of Scottish rhapsody, a romantically partisan prose poem of a land that never was by a visitor who had gathered impressions instead of facts, an evocation of Edinburgh brooding on blood and history and of Glasgow sinking in pride and despair. Here and there, from the cracks as it were, a mouse-nose of story peeked out. Some sense of reality took over; out went Edinburgh entire, taking the brooding romanticism with it, followed by most of the Glasgow description, until all that was left was the little grid of streets round George Square and Glasgow Green, the essential theatres of action. With the surplus scenery cleared away the action proceeded with proper speed.

At once a new problem arose. The science fiction ambience had changed. Recession costs and prices were menacing every operator, from writer to bookseller. Most reviewers had treated *Beloved Son* as a serious novel, which had been pleasing, but common sense suggested that under the new conditions there would be little room for a second book on the same expansive lines. A more immediate reminder was Faber's unwillingness to entertain another work of such costly length now that they had a fair idea of my earning potential, which did not seem to be high. Against this, I had over a couple of years built up my examination of the extended life theme to the point where a much *longer* novel was needed to expound it thoroughly.

What to do? The obvious answer was *Drop the idea and write something else*, and a more practically minded writer might have done that. And rightly so; a man who writes for his living doesn't necessarily bow completely to market forces but neither does he deliberately set himself in opposition to them. Unwilling to discard so much preparation, I looked for a middle course and found a perilous one.

There are, broadly speaking, two main modes of transmitting a complex idea in fiction. One is to lay it out, not too explicitly, in scenes designed to express this facet or that, which is what I had done at leisure in *Beloved Son*; this mode requires considerable wordage and a reader willing to concentrate. The other is to devise characters who represent the essential facets of the idea to be conveyed and set them in situations where the statements are implied so strongly that even the superficial reader will not need further explanation.

The second is an unsubtle method agape with pitfalls, one that a few unwary practitioners have termed the 'literary thriller' and lived to regret it. It is an oil-and-water mixture needing a very smooth emulsifier, and even so is likely to end either as an imperfectly realized novel with raucous elements of the thriller or as a lifeless thriller aping the manners of a novel.

It was this trap-infested area I proposed to enter rather than drop the too-grand conception. Barnum was right about one being born every minute.

Despite Barnum, *Vaneglory* turned out reasonably well. The limitation on wordage worked in favour of taut storytelling and the need for concentration ruled out the fringe grotesques of characterization used in the earlier novel.

The hybrid format was intended to be basically an entertainment from which a few meditations on human aspirations could be extracted by those who cared to look for them.

My main worry was the possibility of an editorial demand that I rewrite the Scottish dialogue, reducing local colour to the occasional 'och' or 'the noo' conventionally used to denote Scottishness in the manner of a stage direction that would not disturb the reader. No such request came; there was, after all, not such a forbidding amount of it and the publisher, Charles Monteith, is a Scot. (However, I see now that it was a mistake; no amount of phonetic fiddling can reproduce the *sound* of a national speech.)

The only complaint came in a concerned note from Carl Routledge, who felt that if I must write science fiction I should produce space opera, under a *nom de plume* if necessary, and make some money. My feeling, then and now, is that space opera does not often make any money beyond the miserable publisher's advance for such work and that in any case I would do it so badly that no-one would want it. Writing space opera, even on the grandest scale, would bore me stiff.

But Charles Monteith received the book with a joy that still seemed immoderate after the proper fifty per cent reduction for professional overkill. I began to believe him when I saw the new contract offering an advance of 2000 pounds (about A$3800 at the time), a fantastic increase on the usual English base rate of about 300 pounds. Sale of paperback rights to Sphere came almost at once, as did sale of Dutch translation rights, again to Prisma. *Ah, frabjous day,* etc.

Then the blight descended.

David Hartwell, who according to one literary agent would 'take another Turner novel yesterday', refused *Vaneglory* for Pocket Books. It is always difficult to discover the 'why' behind a publisher's refusal; it is usually couched in blandly form-letter terms—'not find a place in our list at the present time'—and the readers' reports, which could be helpful and revealing, are guarded from the writer's sight. It came to me in roundabout way that

Hartwell disliked my handling of the female characters.

As a novelist I don't pay much attention to sexist, racist, élitist and other -ist complaints; my characters are selected for the roles required by the theme, and those who dislike this are free to read those writers who run from every possible cause of reader alienation.

Still, as a novelist who would rather sell than not, I recognized that the Hartwell refusal could have some dire consequences, and it did. *Beloved Son* had not been such a marked success in America that other publishers would rush to pick up the option Hartwell dropped; also, since it was in some sense a sequel to the earlier book, nobody would want to print a sequel refused by the publisher of the original work.

That is one of the ways in which a promising future can vanish overnight. It must have dismayed Faber, who would have counted on the American sale to defray some of the large advance they had paid me, and the backlash there would surely show in a smaller advance for the next novel. (It did.)

Vaneglory received a reasonably appreciative press both at home and abroad, but not the praise that had greeted its predecessor. In Australia an unexpectedly warm review from John McLaren (not a science fiction man) in *Overland* eased other disappointments.

The crying poor mouth from England became insistent and one could not blame the criers. The publishing trade was suffering hard times and the fiction branch was becoming reduced to the status of shabby panhandler. Carl wrote that I must work at still shorter length because a long book had to be a pre-sold success to pay for itself, and nothing I wrote (though, kindly, he did not spell it out) was likely to be that.

So *Yesterday's Men*, envisioned on fairly generous lines, had to be reconsidered; even the 'literary thriller' approach, which had worked reasonably well, would be too expansive for what I had in mind. This was a purely technical problem for which an answer could be found. The answer I settled on was to write it as a straight adventure story with only minimum wordage allotted to exposition; psychological and philosophical points would have to remain implicit or even sub-textual, taking their chance of being understood or noticed at all.

When it was done a final worry remained: with the American market pretty certainly closed to the book, Faber might not risk publication in an increasingly straitened market. The situation could scarcely have looked less promising.

Faber, however, did take it and the book came out in 1983, to be greeted by a screech of fury from Damien Broderick in the Melbourne *Age* and a much more thoughtful and encouraging notice in the *London Review of Books*. The extremes of reaction were to the fore again. There is a crumb of comfort to be taken from that, for I have a feeling, hard to rationalize but welcome in a field where comfort is often needed, that when opinions differ so violently about my work I must be getting *something* right. The infuriated reader is paying as much attention, though of a different kind, as the satisfied one.

And that's all there is to tell in the way of warnings and object lessons. There isn't any climax as in a properly made novel; life is too untidy to fall in with the structural needs of fiction and it tends to peter out into inconsequentialities best represented by *ad infinitum* or simply . . .

But I haven't spent so many years hovering round science fiction to have nothing left to say about that.

PART THREE
FOR THOSE IN PERIL . . .

'Millions for entertainment, not one cent for entropy!'
    Gully Foyle in
    Alfred Bester's *The Stars My Destination*

Contemporary history is jogging my elbow as I shape this final chapter. Only last week the Federal Treasurer announced the reimposition of an assets test on the age pensions of Australian citizens over seventy, and my imagination leapt from the simple financial reason for the move to the implications science fiction has long been aware of in its complacent fashion. Then, on the night of 20 May 1983, I heard Prime Minister Robert Hawke speak of the future of employment and recommend that people seek new ways of applying their abilities and energies; he mentioned, specifically, cottage industries, with something of the air of a man grateful for any suggestion to throw into a yawning gap. Then I knew that science fiction had hit our Prime Minister squarely between the eyes, whether he reads it or not, because he was thinking like a science fiction writer taking a worried sight on the dangerous, amorphous future and at first finding only the obvious.

A closer look may bring unease to politicians and public alike. A still closer one may begin the production of buffers against shock.

14

Cottage Industry Time?

In *Rataplan* (no. 21), the excellent fanzine published by
Leigh Edmonds in Canberra, appeared this comment from
Bruce Gillespie, long-time editor of *SF Commentary* and
one of the publishers of this book: 'I find that I must disagree with George Turner more and more, even if only
under my breath. George really seems to think it important
to define science fiction and to denounce poor exponents
of the craft. That's all right if you still believe that the
craft is improvable. I don't think that any more.'

It is easy to understand Bruce's feeling that the genre
has reached a dead end in pop nonsense on the one hand
and in more literary finesse than useful content on the
other; the pop writers are making money and the more
literary types are breathing incense from ivory towers. It is
a discouraging scene.

Nevertheless I must disagree with him, and not under
my breath. I think there is a future, nuclear war or no
nuclear war, for all of us and that an intelligent science
fiction can play a present role in examining it.

1. Science Fiction at Tether's End
'All art', wrote Oscar Wilde, making a quotable generalization of a minuscule grain of truth, 'is useless.' But no art is
wholly useless; the worst may be studied with advantage
for what it tells of the society that produced it, and the
most crassly imitative still serves a purpose in disseminating
the great creative ideas to those who might otherwise never
brush against them.

Science fiction has at least a foot in the door of art,

being at its best a powerfully creative medium, but what *use* has it?

Ninety per cent of readers, perhaps more, will mime disgust with the question and ask *Does it have to be useful?* No, it doesn't, and to anyone who can ask the question it surely is useless. Then, since anything useless may as well be done without, is there an argument for its continued existence?

There is, but first it would be well to see how and why it has failed to deliver the promise it displayed nearly a century ago.

Before World War II we knew where we were in Science Fiction Land, as well as when we were. We had not ventured so imaginatively far as to feel emotionally severed from the world we understood; we knew how and why these new fictional surroundings had come into being. Stories held us not only by the spell of wonderment but because the wonderment spoke directly to what we knew, then gave what we knew the twist essential to turning it into what we might know if only we willed it.

This was what J. G. Ballard termed 'the literature of preparation for change', the literature that Hugo Gernsback sought to propagate and nearly destroyed by popularizing it on too low a level, the literature that in the thirties and forties set young minds thinking about possible tomorrows and turned quite a few to the study of real science.

Today's science fiction would scarcely turn a mind to the study of anything, except perhaps Science Fiction As An Irrational Phenomenon.

That would yield poor results because its function as an irrational phenomenon has been taken over by other branches of popular publishing, such as the work of best-selling horror novelists like Stephen King and Peter Straub and others who seek to overwhelm with symbols of psychosexual revulsion (no pretence of catharsis by pity and terror), which science fiction's poor puppet monsters could never match. The monsters were only dreams of the Worlds of Maybe, confrontable and defeatable; the evocations of slaughter and brutality in such recent horror novels as *Lamia* and *Floating Dragon* render the sights of a battlefield reasonable—and I have seen a few battlefields. Science fiction's 'awe and wonder' is child's play by comparison.

At the higher end of the critical scale the more literate and responsible novelists have also reached into science fiction's bag of tricks for fresh effects and, if only because they are in the main finer craftsmen than the genre writers, have exploited them to much greater effect. Science fiction's two major claims to originality have been its presentation of new metaphors for the human condition, drawing them from practical science and theoretical extrapolation, and its ability to evoke reaction by delineating the normal with the 'one small change' that results in a new perspective. Some major novelists have taken over these techniques with powerful imaginative results; in Australia, Rodney Hall's *Just Relations*, David Ireland's *A Woman of the Future*, Gerald Murnane's *The Plains*; in Britain, Christopher Priest's *The Affirmation*, Alasdair Gray's *Lanark*, D. M. Thomas's *Birthstone*; in America, John Gardner's *Mickelsson's Ghosts*, Thomas Pynchon's *Gravity's Rainbow*. These are only a selection of the better known; whether they have literary or intellectual staying power is yet to be shown, but they help to demonstrate that at both ends of the literary scale science fiction has been outplayed with its own special skills.

Where to, then?

Backward a little, I think, to re-examine origins and see what avenues have been passed by—backward as far as Wells to see what tracks he and his contemporaries may have left for us. One at least is plain to see.

In sum, it is time science fiction got back into the prediction business. *Not* the business of predicting technical wonders, which is childishly easy, but the business of asking 'If this goes on, what will be the end?' And not with our present pantheon of reality-avoiding writers; most of them will be incapable of what I have in mind. We need a new breed of science fiction and a new breed of historically and socially educated writer to drag the genre screaming into contact with the facts of life.

2. Propaganda and the Reader

In the time of Bellamy, Verne and Wells, science fiction had a purpose and a target; all three of them made their phenomenally successful ways preaching and teaching the ideas they believed in to a public only too willing to listen.

A critical shibboleth of today's readers, however, is that preaching is out. None of this 'story with a message'! These same readers have gobbled down, in astronomical numbers, the novels of Angry Young Men pointing out what a pack of dispensable pigs human beings are (except the angry ones), of Angry Young Women laying down the law about female rights, of Angry Coloured Men with a leaven of Whites shouting the disgrace of racism, of Young and Old Men and Women turning a more or less honest penny 'exposing' every activity, preferably politico-sexo-steamy-violent, that can be squeezed out of a word processor. Is it possible that they have not noticed that they are being preached at, propagandized? It is quite possible; the perception of propaganda depends upon the inclinations of the reader. If he agrees with the writer's statement, he is reading a fine and useful work whose message he will spread by recommending that you, too, read it; if he disagrees, then he is being fed objectionable propaganda, preached at, offered a message he doesn't want.

'I don't like a story with a message' belongs in the same dustbin as 'I don't like stories in the first person' and 'I can't stand dialect'. The reader's prejudice is overridden if the product gratifies other areas of his taste.

The fact is that the story without a meaning—that is, some form of message, whether overt or not and whether the reader accepts it or not—is worth neither writing nor reading except as a transient, immediately forgettable entertainment.

Observe here the reader in action, happily oblivious of what he thinks he dislikes:

The three most influential science fiction novels, in terms of their public impact, have been Bellamy's *Looking Backward* (which outsold *Uncle Tom's Cabin* in its day and is still in print), Huxley's *Brave New World* (which

206

outraged a generation in 1932 and is still in print) and Orwell's *1984*, which we no longer need to read because its Newspeak, surveillance and brain washing have become part of our received knowledge of the world.

They were novels that set out, with conscious intent, to preach, the first to pass the message of the socialist paradise, the others to say 'Watch out, you are heading for trouble.' Socialism has lost its paradisal aspects but the other two came uncomfortably close to the direction of contemporary social evolution. Nobody reading them complained about being preached at; they were too busy either praising or vilifying the sermon to complain of didacticism. The books did what was intended of them: they made people take notice. And they sold in hundreds of thousands.

Science fiction is a stuffed well of popular preachments: Bradbury's *Fahrenheit 451* cried out against censorship of ideas; Ballard has been telling us for years to get rid of the past and start afresh; Le Guin has been openly laying out simple diagrams of argument to express a point of view; the late Philip K. Dick made a career of trying to convince us of the existence of realities beyond the immediately perceptible; Heinlein has been blowing the trumpets of imperialism over decades as well as advocating forms of serial marriage that add up to an all-in family love-fest. Nobody seems to mind, save for an occasional squawk at Heinlein's descent into dullness.

All these are successful writers who push their barrows blatantly and powerfully. The message-haters lap up their works without a quiver of inconsistency.

Most of the more respected science fiction writers operate from a soapbox (while denying it fearfully if accused); some conceal it, some do not. Think of Lem, Disch, Sladek, the Strugatskis, Watson, Russ—the list goes on and on.

These are among the most considerable genre authors in terms of influence on useful academic interest and on the directions of the genre itself—meaning, finally, on the reading public. They are the writers whom the hacks plunder for ideas to trivialize. They are, however altered the detail of their individual approaches, in the tradition of More, Bacon, Wells and Huxley.

They preach. And they are read by shoals of those people who can't bear fiction with a message.

The shame is that their abilities are being more and more confined in a genre building ivory towers. Not that the ivory-tower-builders haven't a great right on their side; I would not want to be without the persuasive involvements of Gene Wolfe, the 'End of Time' stories of Michael Moorcock or the oddities and quiddities of the thought of Brian Aldiss; the landscape would be drearier in their absence. But they remain the expert players with fancies, the decorators of mental scenes we already know; they give the world a flick and a polish, or stand it now and then on its head, but move not a step beyond its easy dreams. They are no longer science fiction writers but fantasists; they are in flight.

There is room and a need for a new kind of science fiction writer, one with a willingness to study the social crises building up to bedevil the next two generations, and with the creative power to present simple cases, not to the intelligentsia and the literati, but to the wide romance-reading public, which is usually unaware of the falling axe until the blade is in its neck.

It is time, as the saying has it, to get down to the nitty-gritty. Just what are these matters that should be occupying our futurologists?

A few are obvious, and every reader is at least peripherally aware of them as something he will have to give thought to, some time or other—if the TV breaks down and he has to get back into thought and conversation.

First, however, a quick look at the failures of science fiction as a predictive agent, and a suggestion of the attitudes of mind that caused them.

3. *Comfortable Ideas and Painless Solutions*
Through most of its early existence science fiction concerned itself with technical wonders whose achievement seemed inevitable, and in due course most of them

appeared. But never quite in the forms predicted by the writers. Seen by an eager public as having a predictive function, science fiction seemed simple-minded when the realities appeared.

Television was prominent among early predictions, but rarely bruited as more than an adjunct to the telephone, which it has notably *not* become, save in a few closed-circuit uses; that it could and would alter the domestic habits of the planet as well as its cultural responses to matters of fact and fiction never occurred to the authors. They thought in romantic terms rather than in terms of the responses of the common man or, more influentially, the business man.

The space flight dream antedated the television dream but, almost until the launching of the first satellite, authors thought of spaceships as artefacts to be built by passably rich men in backyard workshops and operated as casually as motor cars; the immensity of the projects never entered their minds because they had neither the knowledge nor the vision to appreciate the difficulties. They did not think in practical terms, such as money and research and centralized expertise.

The fissioned atom appeared in the twenties with a wonderful nonchalance; many in the thirties were still arming their heroes with atom-powered hand-guns! Even Wells, who knew his way around the sciences, did not in *The World Set Free* envision the true awesomeness of Little Boy and its successors. Wells saw such destructive power as the inevitable precursor of peace under the fear of extinction. The present-day version of that dream, though in retrospect obvious, seems to have occurred to no-one. So much of science fiction's optimism has been predicated on humanity's ultimate goodwill and good sense. (Lately the genre has been accused rather of pessimism, as though that were a weakness. Is optimism necessarily more clear-eyed?)

All things considered, the predictive writers rarely hit a useful mark and never realized the possibilities when they did land the occasional lucky guess. By the end of World War II they were sufficiently sensible of this to disclaim the predictive function save in the broadest terms. Aware

209

of their inability to make more than random stabs at a future daily overtaking them by the exponentially increasing speed of technological advance, they turned to the postulation of vast changes at a safe distance in time, but rarely, if ever, did they consider the historical processes by which these changes came about. The fictive attitude became a playful *What if?* when what was needed, is still needed, is a thoughtful *If this goes on . . .*

Given the enormous amount of science fiction written from the fifties onwards, the reason for this is easily seen: social/technological/philosophical change *in action*, caught so to speak on the wing, is simply too difficult for the untrained dreamer to correlate and follow. (Arthur C. Clarke is a trained dreamer of today's product, but he too keeps historical processes well out of the way and prefers the *fait accompli*; his futures have all their major problems solved so that he can get on with the pipe dreams.) The average writer can hazard a guess at where a particular trend will lead or what answer will emerge to a specific cultural problem, but the wider implications of change will escape him, operating beyond the limits of his thinking, or seem too complex to embody in a work of reasonable length that will also be intelligible to readers no better equipped than himself.

So the novelist ignores the real problem, which is the how and why of transition, and writes about the possible end product, with no indication of how it might be arrived at.

The results are often intriguing and more often empty. By 2033, writes X, all sexist and racist questions will have been solved, allowing him to offer us a smoothly operating world—passing silently over a planetful of urgent and imminent crises that make his thesis at best difficult of accomplishment, at worst naïve or despotic. Or, by 2075 the World State is in operation, presiding over universal peace, but the horrendous problems to be solved in setting up and maintaining such a politically unlikely organization have been passed over as having somehow sorted themselves out. Or, by 2116 the human life span has been increased to an average two centuries, with seven or eight generations of a family living at the one time—but not a word about population pressures, multiple generation gaps, resource difficulties or the cultural revolutions necessary to support such a vast range of educations and experiences.

Science fiction today displays goodwill rather than good sense; it leaps over the too-hard basket to bound straight into the Never-Never Land of Problems Solved.

The argument immediately presents itself that it has never been required of the novelist that he solve the world's problems, that his business is to point them out and discuss them. It is precisely here that science fiction fails to justify its existence; the mainstream, armed with modern techniques, does much better in helping the reader to understand his world. Science fiction neither points out nor discusses; there is a distinct pretence that the real world is of little importance.

Such writing can hardly be regarded as preparation for change, so its last remaining constructive value may no longer hold.

The situation is in fact not quite so debilitated; the promulgation of easy solutions to formidable problems helps to keep the predicaments in the public eye—the eye of that broad-based public to whom the specialized works of scientists, statisticians and philosophers are meaningless or inaccessible. There is some importance in spreading awareness of the immense changes that will face us in the next generation or two; it is not so important that easy solutions be canvassed as that there be an appreciation of the changes—moral, political, industrial, financial, domestic, psychological—that must be prepared for if we are to come through with as little mental and spiritual harm as possible.

Science fiction can play a small role here if ever it ceases to regard itself at one extreme as a set of rarefied exercises in philosophy, metaphysics or increasingly tired satire, or at the other, as mindless escapism. A middle course—consideration of change in terms of contemporary preparation and understanding—could direct attention to the realities of cultural evolution and revolution, where at present it peddles only dreams of success or nightmares of destruction.

The nature of a socially meaningful role for the genre can be clarified by examining some of the recognized

hurdles to tomorrow against some of the fictional over-
leapings of them. It will pay to look first at the most
urgent of present difficulties, because failure to deal with
it will eliminate all the others at a stroke.

4. Nuclear Brinkmanship

To be or not to be is a more urgent question than Shakespeare could possibly have imagined, and taking up arms
against a sea of troubles is admitted to be the surest way
of going out with an almighty bang and a final self-pitying
whimper. Nuclear deterrent and the continuing arguments
about it seem to be our only immediate shield against
obliteration, but this is the Age of Hysteria, when a single
idiot in the wrong place at the wrong time can bring the
whole of history down in ruins.

The science-fictional approaches to this urgent problem
make a fine collection of oddities:

(a) The most common is the simple brazen cop-out,
wherein the story is set so far in the future that the whole
matter is by then over and done with, lost in history, no
longer worth mentioning; this is the method of pretending
it will go away if you don't look at it. Optimism is a
desirable trait, but deadly when it refuses to recognize
dangers.

(b) A World State is postulated, on the understanding
that this would at once wipe out regional and cultural
enmities and usher in universal peace. (It wouldn't.) This is
a wholly optimistic solution to which the author feels no
reasonable objection can be raised; it is in fact so naïve
that few reasonable questions can be asked. I postulated a
limited form of World Government in my three post-
holocaust novels, mainly to illustrate such an organization's
inability to deal successfully with regional and cultural
tensions save in terms of despotism and corrupt double-
dealing.

(c) The inevitability of global holocaust is accepted,
with the preservation of a nucleus of people to repopulate
the planet. This is a not impossible outline of future
history, but few writers face up to examination of the re-
building process (Russell Hoban, in *Riddley Walker*, is a
fine exception); most prefer to maunder on about mutant

212

monsters (few of which would in fact grow to maturity) or skip a few centuries—and the difficulties—as in Approach (a).

(d) The deterrent stand-off is ended when one major nation or the other (depending on the nationality of the writer) invents a device protective against radiation and nuclear weapons. This is usually called a 'force field', which is a safe term because nobody knows what on earth it might mean. This is the Easy Miracle approach, but in an era of galloping technology it should not be altogether discarded; it no longer pays to snort 'Impossible!' when just around the corner someone may be proving you wrong. The objection to this wish-fulfilment wand-waving is that it would represent a postponement, not a solution. The next project would be nullification of the force field.

(e) Approach (e) is for fantasy buffs with fairy godmothers. In this one a benevolent alien pays a visit, nullifies our armaments and in some fashion establishes enduring peace. In the more realistic versions we kill him, demonstrating that we are irredeemable and don't deserve peace, or don't know what to do with it, or just don't like it. This, of course, may be true, in which case we may as well plant a few cobalt bombs to cover the planet and get the business over with. (There are other fantasy approaches; the reader is welcome to all of them.)

Science fiction cannot be blamed for the inconclusiveness of these ideas; the concerned communities of scientists, soldiers and politicians have produced nothing better. If anyone is to be congratulated it should be, to the astonishment of all, the politicians, who have kept doomsday at bay by talking their heads off to each other across the bargaining tables while terrorism, small wars, greed and stupidity light fires round their feet. I know no more than they an easy counter to the danger of racial suicide, but I feel that science fiction, of all the popular literatures, might have attempted some justification of itself as an intellectual mode by at least making some tentative assessments.

Disarmament and pacifism can provide breathing spaces but they cannot still the conflicts and passions arising from racism, starvation, financial greed, personal aggrandizement, religious and cultural intolerance, political manoeuvring and the infinitude of abrasions that mark personal and international relationships. These must be laid to rest before the planet can breathe freely.

How? That won't be known until we understand how and why violence, both physical and mental, plays so large a part in our psychology—and how to control it as an exact psychological exercise.

An immediate and reasonable demurrer might be that man without aggressiveness or the capacity for violence would be at a biological dead end, a cow grazing on the universe, prey to the first aggressor to evolve within reach of him, but I don't postulate removal of the forces that brought us up from the caves. The stance taken in my three science fiction novels, all of which have the same underlying theme, is that we have reached the point where as a race we must understand ourselves or risk suicide by ignorance. I believe with T. S. Eliot that 'It is not enough to understand what we ought to be, unless we know what we are.'* I used that sentence as an epigraph to *Yesterday's Men*, which spells out the statement in detail, though the novelistic metaphor may be judged unsubtle. We must understand the nature of aggression and learn to harness it for constructive purposes. Until we do so we will shudder between deterrence and pacifism, and suffer the consequences of unrelieved stress. Human culture is already notably paranoid, and a deep-seated paranoia is one of the most intractable of mental conditions. Ask your friendly psychiatrist.

My approach begs as many questions as it answers, but it is not offered as a solution, only as a suggestion of where the solution might lie; it would require many people of rare talent and training to investigate and foster it.

There may be, surely are, other solutions, and there is room in the more responsible areas of science fiction for discussion of them on the level of the common reader. The

* T. S. Eliot, 'Religion and Literature', in *Selected Essays* (London: Faber and Faber, 1932/1951), p. 399.

214

more the common man and woman can be convinced that rational resolutions of our dilemmas are possible, the more chance there will be that capable intelligences will turn to the consideration of such resolutions, however unlikely at first glance, and the more chance that unexpected and radical conceptions will come to light.

Dissemination of ideas via science fiction may not at first seem to amount to much, but I pointed out in the opening chapter of this book that the genre's penetration of daily life is deep and broad; it reaches into every aspect of living. Nor would it do the genre any harm as a literary arm to adopt a responsible attitude to the real burdens of that real world it professes to dissect and criticize and hold up to satire. We might find a new division of science fiction into 'responsible' and 'irresponsible', 'aware' and 'featherbrained'.

5. The Shape of the Automated Paradise

Science fiction, busy with Utopia and Dystopia, has never looked more than cursorily at the rugged road to either; rarely considering the means of achieving world peace, it has also ignored the consequences.

Demilitarization and pacifism demand the elimination of all armaments. Questions intimately connected with the shape of the future at once arise. What will be done with the tens of millions of men and women whose livelihoods will vanish with the dissolution of the world's armed forces? The idea of alternative employment for them would be a black joke. And what will be the effect of shutting down the armaments trade? There is a glib answer: small arms-buying countries will save huge slices of national revenue while those that sell them may find themselves in a lightning recession from which only a change of cultural mores will save them—oh! good, good! But the effect on thousands of dependent industries would be catastrophic and soon felt by every person alive; peace on Earth would be an immense boost to unemployment, and this financial aspect could be a major political factor affecting the question: Peace or eternal brinkmanship?

The problem of retrenched servicemen and armament

215

workers would be only an exacerbation of the greater problem of the disposition of an almost totally retrenched working class, possibly within a generation, surely within two. Prime Minister Hawke's 'cottage industries' reference was only a pale recognition of the coming task.

It has been calculated that the world's productive output, from mining and agriculture to secondary manufacture, will by AD 2000 be capable of being handled by 2 per cent of the available workforce. Desperate trade unions, and governments rightly terrified by a soaring social services bill, will try to hold up the automated take-over, but technology will roll over them because cost reductions are necessary to perpetuate the myth of an infinitely expanding industrial market. But, if no-one earns, who buys?

'Cottage industries' and makework programs will not hold the line for long; there is no more dispirited worker than the one who knows that what he is doing is useless, that a machine can do it faster as well as better, that his place as a useful member of society is held on sufferance and that his wage is a euphemism for charity. Yet, being human (a condition implying wanting to eat the cake and have it), he will demand the leisure-and-comfort benefits promised by the new technology, but will also demand an income wherewith to pay for them. But if the technology has removed his power to earn? This is the common man's ultimate no-win situation, not necessarily over-simplified in summary.

The price of social services, which we have been raised to regard as ours by right, is mounting at a rate that in a decade or two could be beyond the capacity of any treasury to pay. That, in turn, is the price of health and longevity, another looming monster.

A new society, founded on a different view of supply and demand, of status and responsibility, of use and relegation, of expectation and aspiration, must emerge. But what type of society? Science fiction, nimbly leaping the vital transition period, has opted for the starry-eyed and obvious—when, that is, it has paused to recognize the problem at all.

The popular suggestion is for the adoption of a universal

social credit scheme whereby every individual has a government-guaranteed minimum credit (share of the wealth) established at birth and calculated to support him/her in necessities throughout life. Personal qualities and useful abilities would determine his/her capacity to earn additional credit in a fiercely competitive and narrow market. There are superficial attractions in this idea—for those who fancy living in regimented material equality under a total bureaucracy—until it is realized that distribution of wealth and resources to provide worldwide subsistence would not raise Third World existence to the plush level of the American or even the European standard, but would drag the entire planet down to something approaching the present Third World condition. Only large-scale starvation allows small-scale luxury, and the hungry multiply by the minute.

The situation could eventually be alleviated (obvious points of attack are improved distribution, recycling and simpler life-styles) but the chances are that millennia of culture would be warped and fractured in the process. *Something* has to give. Perhaps a painless approach to a workless culture is possible; if so, science fiction in its dreams of tomorrow has not thought of it. Nor, so far as I know, has any other organ; generations of disaster could be the end of thought delayed too long.

Science fiction's naïve fixation on far futures might be more usefully focused nearer to today; it just might throw up a valid thought to contribute to the revolutionary situations to come. If scientists, economists, politicians, psychologists and the humanitarian groups looked up from their specialized areas of concern to observe the aspect of the coming storm, they might concede that the hand-to-mouth approach has run out of time and that hard consensus thinking is an urgent need.

The workless culture will come, no doubt of that, but care will be needed to ensure that it comes as a benefit rather than as another struggle up from the ruins.

It will be noticed that the foregoing meditation is predicated on a *world* effort to come through in as good condition as possible. But is a world effort to be expected? Or will those countries with some prospect of self-sufficiency—

e.g. the USA, Russia, Australia, China, Brazil—lock their frontiers and tough it out on a policy of isolationism, of first look after your own and let the rest do as they can?

As a scenario it is not beyond possibility. In this century humanity has established records in genocide, so a turning of backs on misery should present few problems.

This brings us to consideration of the right to life.

6. The Right to Life

Anti-abortionists and right-to-lifers flourish in a world whose 'civilized' values give no more honest thought to anyone's right to be born or to stay alive than did the hordes of Genghis Khan. Round the world great nations and small nod weary lip-service and continue killing. So much for right.

The cheapening of life is guaranteed by starvation, as a by-product of war and/or depletion of resources, or as simple neglect, also by the paranoid fear ingrained in governments incapable of preserving their tenure save by extermination of the opposition. A powerful guarantee is the sheer size of the planet's population, which stands at about 4500 million at the time of writing, and at the present rate of increase could reach 14,000 million by AD 2050, with the children of today's teenagers taking the impact.

Science fiction has canvassed such forecasts but has offered few confrontations with them. Probably the best known of the few, Harry Harrison's *Make Room! Make Room!*, had only conventional warnings to give and, like Robert Silverberg's *The World Inside*, was concerned with regimentation and discipline rather than with under-standing what these conditions might do to the group mentality. Both helped to demonstrate that science fiction is given to jackboot answers to social problems: it reflects the world's administrative thinking on repressive neces-sities but rarely questions it. As usual, it skips the working out and goes straight to the intuitive answers; then it skips consideration of the practicability of the answers.

One group of fictive future-watchers plunges straight into the morass of overpopulation without thought of a transition period of preventive or palliative attempts; the other hops directly to an idyllic tomorrow when the ugly growing pains are past and done with and one can get on with more tractable imaginings. The second group has nothing useful to say but the horror scenarios of the first have wide acceptance:

(a) In the most wholesale forecast (very long range) the world has become a vast city where swarming billions live in something close to a slave state. The power wielders live on the top levels in the sunlight; the rest spawn sullenly in the metal caverns. All food is synthetic. A commonplace of such tales is the discovery of a single tree, miraculously preserved, which stuns the discoverer with awe and wonder. The writers of such might have done better to do some wondering for themselves—about atmospheric conditions and food supply on a planet denuded of growth. The silliness of this vision lies in its failure to recognize the tragedy of a non-ecology wherein man alone inhabits the Earth (in some versions he infests the sea as well), and its equal failure to ask how this stage was reached without cultural breakdown. The view of the world as a cheek-by-jowl psychological and physical slum is surprisingly prevalent, a failure of novelistic nerve on a dismaying scale. The right to life is preserved at the expense of all quality of life.

(b) World population, in more conservative scripts, has been stabilized by the enforcement of some such decree as limitation of progeny to one per couple. This leads at once to the idea of limiting conception to those who will produce children of a standard calculated to improve the race. (Shaw's famous question to Mrs Patrick Campbell—'What if it had my body and your brains?'—makes a suitable gloss for this possibility.) It makes a fine vision of élitist stratification and loss of cultural homogeneity, and in it the jackboot mentality is coolly stirring. Yet there will have to be, sooner or later, a measure of restraint—meaning, restraining measures. How may this be done without damaging a race whose psychology is built around conception and whose continuance is guaranteed by maximization of genetic interchange? We can't risk many more such areas of mental stress before neurotic man becomes psychotic man. So where stands individual right to life against the need for quality of life?

(c) The food problem gets a little fringe attention, mostly on the understanding that the scientists will sort it out. Given goodwill and a proper distribution system, starvation need not exist today, and possibly should not exist even in the conditions of the mid-twenty-first century. This planet, properly farmed and conserved, could feed more than twenty thousand million people. Whether it could at the same time provide anything else but food, or support any species besides man, is a moot point that science fiction files under Too Hard. However, some aspects of the food problem attract the ghouls. Many writers have solved the future food problem by cannibalism, and in stress situations it is always a possible solution. It is also one that, practised on a large scale purely for sustenance and without the ritual connotations that absolved the cannibal communities of guilt, might have a considerable psychological backlash. But, as the film *Soylent Green* suggested without seeming to offend anyone's sensibilities, it will be all right so long as you don't *know* what is disguised in your daily ration biscuit. Sooner or later someone will ask why death shouldn't actively serve the right to life.

(d) One really baroque idea for stabilizing population growth is the encouragement of homosexuality as a sex substitute with no drawback of breeding; it pops up often in the literature. How heterosexuals might be persuaded to change their erotic spots defies my imagination; homosexual couplings among the heterosexually deprived, as in prisons, do not represent a change of life-style but a temporary and not wholly satisfactory accommodation, terminated on return to society. The psychological repercussions of such mass manipulation could be shattering or laughable. If in some extraordinary manner the attempt succeeded the results could be catastrophic. Adaptation to changing conditions is possibly painful but ultimately successful; forcible topping and tailing to fit an environment is likely to provide more disasters than it avoids.

These scenarios may be in detail ridiculous, but the political picture emerging from them is less so. It is predominantly fascist, involving in its most extreme form a pyramidal power structure with a small apical plateau of the super-powerful resting on an authority base formed by a technology-backed police force of obedient automata, who kill with no questions asked by or of the killers; the vast mass of the people is totally regimented in thought, controlled in movement, starved of activity beyond contemplation of a whole-wall Tri-V screen and fed on laboratory-synthesized foods. Somewhere in the cellars of this world lurks a ratlike criminal element displaying the only free thought in a mentally comatose society; why an all-powerful police state cannot eradicate them by simple slaughter, no questions asked, is never explained. That such a picture goes unquestioned by readers may be interpreted as a frightening admission that this simple-minded conform-or-be-killed future is the one they accept as a prime probability.

It is worth noting that another great area of popular fiction, the political thriller of espionage and cloak-and-dagger, presents a startling contemporary version of the origins of such a world. This area concentrates on power struggle, typically with a ruthless group, often of businessmen or scientists, seeking to seize and maintain unchallenged authority by subversion or murder; sometimes the opposition comes from a similar group, sometimes from government agents—the single hero-figure is less prominent today. The effects of these private wars on the general public are rarely considered; people are targets, manipulated and disposable. The reader is placated with an ending wherein virtue (meaning the side presented sympathetically by the author, though there is often little moral difference between the contestants) triumphs, and in the excitement may never notice that he, the uncommitted reader, is the prototype of the disregarded public. This type of fiction, often written with great skill, contributes however unintentionally to the conditioning of its readership to acceptance of a world picture in which power is stolen and bartered over its thrill-fascinated head, and in which it plays no part in determining its own future.

The science fiction writers are portraying the end

221

result of activities nurtured by the mainstream yarn spinners.

And the right to life? Science fiction says little about it, and that little tends to infer that life has always been cheap and that as unchecked population growth turns the planet into a cosmic slum it will become cheaper.

Can we build a possible scenario based on the year 2023 when (The Bomb permitting) a planetary population of nine thousand million could be a fact? This may represent the feasible limit of human numbers for the planet or even be beyond it when feasibility is worked out in terms of resource exhaustion, air pollution, heat pollution, soil pollution and the breakdown of those environmental balances governing weather, soil fertility, the CO_2 level of the air and the self-cleaning capacities of rivers and the ocean.

Restriction of population will have to be implemented on a planetwide basis. China and India show us what to expect and guard against: from China comes sub-vocal reports of exposure of girl children so that permission for another child may bring the desired boy, while in India the vasectomy program seems to have fathered coercion of the ignorant and corruption of the administrators. Human venality seems ineradicable; given the same circumstances, Western nations are not likely to behave any better. Who gives a damn for the future of the race when there is present gain to be siphoned off?

So what of AD 2023, when the choices could be abstention, contraception, abortion or conception by state permission? All these represent denial of life, which worries the Roman Catholic Church as well as other honestly concerned people; they also represent wide-scale denial of some part of the psychological basis of living, the denial, distortion and curtailment of psychobiological demands.

There will also be the burden of the aged. Again science fiction has little to say on the matter; only Sumner Locke Elliott, in *Going*, has presented bluntly a picture of people being killed off at an age determined by statute, though a few short stories have handled it sentimentally. The aged will be a financial impossibility long before the food runs short; by 2013 they could muster seventy per cent of the population, more if medicine continues its triumphant leaps and bounds.

There is no need to spell out the means of disposing of society's surplus; let us simply not pretend that dreams of the right to life will play any part in them. Humanity, which knows about culling over-fecund species, will be the first to face the trauma of culling itself. And a cull is not a one-off operation; it must be continuous. Let the powerless beware!

There can be no question of avoiding some form of cull; the question is one of convincing a biologically driven humanity that it must learn restraint, and of compensating for the resultant psychological losses. It needs study now, not in thirty years time.

Humanity faces, in the next half century, not a crisis but a constellation of crises, and science fiction, which once had a genuine concern for the future, has scarcely a word to say about encroaching realities. It is the one genuinely optimistic branch of twentieth-century literature, the only one that believes that if you don't look, whatever it is will go away.

It would be idle to pretend that a responsible science fiction could answer the bitter questions waiting, but it could begin the process of laying out, in dramatic form, the need for thought and the areas of need. Its largest readership is among today's young, who will live to face the consequences of present thoughtlessness. Some thinking should begin in a genre specifically designed, in its origins, to foster thought.

Even Prime Minister Hawke's throwaway reference to cottage industries was an uneasy recognition that somewhere and soon the run of the lemmings has to stop, but it won't even slow down unless understanding of future dangers becomes general in the world. The poor, with little to lose, will be the hardest to convince.

These forecasts are all too classically simple to come to pass precisely as here suggested; neither history nor humanity is so accurately assessable, and so-called 'futurology' is about as much a science as teacup reading. There will be stopgaps and holding measures and false starts;

there will be unforeseen developments that will change the course of events overnight, to introduce wholly new options—and dangers.

Still, these menacing factors will play a strangling role in our social evolution, and there should be planning against the obvious. Sir Macfarlane Burnet, who has given much thought to tomorrow, has said that we must plan for 'five years ahead, and twenty years, and a hundred years', and that seems a plain enough statement of the need. One might think of his divisions as five years, perhaps, for stop-gap solutions to give breathing space while great transitions are planned, twenty years to prepare these plans against the impact of sweeping change, and a hundred years to do what we can to ensure that yet more distant generations are not presented with a legacy of rolling catastrophe. It is too late to cling to any belief that we, as a race, will muddle through. If we were indeed one race that might happen, but we are not; we are a jigsaw of cultures pulling in different directions, with consensus little more than a talking-point for politicians applying band-aids.

The natures of the five, twenty and hundred years plans will not be easily decided, but any that do not take into account nationalistic paranoia, automation, population pressure, increased leisure and progressive environmental destruction (plus such lethal fringe items as education and corruption) will be rolled over by a relentless reality.

7. A Small Role for Science Fiction

If science fiction writers were asked to study genuine possibilities and make forceful fiction of them, most would offer a bland smile and murmur that prediction is not really their business.

But speculation surely is. Some of them insist that 'SF' stands for Speculative Fiction; this gets rid of that awkward word 'science' and replaces it with one so vague that they can take the universe for a playground without recognition of restraints and realities. Given such freedom, few bother to speculate; they merely imagine.

Who, then, could write a popular fiction based on logical

scenarios for the near future? Certainly not too many of the present authors. Science and reality are actively resented by many of them; they get in the way, spoil the plots, invalidate the premises, shouldn't really exist. Science, wrote Christopher Priest in *SF Commentary*, belongs in *New Scientist*.

A more subtle rejection came from Brian Aldiss, who wrote in *Billion Year Spree* that Hugo Gernsback's emphasis on the need for scientific accuracy in the stories he published 'had the effect of introducing a deadening literalism into the fiction'. (I wonder, does he regard Arthur C. Clarke's extensive use of science in his fiction as deadening literalism?) The truth, which anyone can test by reading a few issues of these old magazines, is that the deadening was the product of a dreary lack of fictive talent among Gernsback's contributors.

Science fiction was in the hands of amateurs in 1926 and later fell into the hands of pulp hacks; by the time a few real talents appeared the 'scientific' aspect of the genre was observed by only a small group of writers.

In fiction any approach is legitimate; an author must write as he chooses. It is simply a pity that a promising tool has been subjugated to the spinning of fairy-floss, and the one usefulness setting it apart from other fiction discarded.

Science as an ingredient requires thought, a little not-too-arduous research and a touch of genuinely extrapolative imagination if it is to be used productively in fiction. The same applies to sociological speculation. If these are to be integrated into fiction, in simple terms requiring no special knowledge on the part of the reader, there is need for a flexible technique, one that can make its point without labouring. Few writers have met this challenge; Wells and Beresford did it in their day, as did Sinclair Lewis in *Martin Arrowsmith*, while Verne and Bellamy could not; among the moderns Le Guin succeeds, as do the Strugatskis, while Gregory Benford does not. Few others so much as try, and in consequence their stories become ephemeras that have lost touch with reality. The few genre stories that have outlived their initial publication and received general acclaim have been notably aware of reality and hardheaded about mere fantasizing.

A new style of science fiction writer is needed, one who will ignore trends and conventional ideas and predigested reader requirements, and find for a disintegrating genre a fresh reason for its existence.

He will need to be one who thinks the work worth doing for its own sake. He will not be writing works of art—at any rate not at first—but solid, tradesmanlike fiction with a purpose, overt or covert. If he does it well, the readers won't give a damn whether or not it is didactic; if he touches chords of recognition in them, they will read him. In this area a great technician may at first do more useful work than a great artist. The technicians commonly precede the artists, establishing the bases from which a new creativity springs.

The new author would not be writing science fiction as fans and publishers understand the term; he would be using the techniques to write political fiction; he would be preparing, whether bluntly or subtly, those mental buffers which Ballard had in mind when he called science fiction 'the literature of preparation for change'. People can always be reached through their preferred entertainment; that is the great lesson of the PR trade.

Commercialized science fiction could and would carry on mass production, and a more aesthetic science fiction would continue to play with metaphysics and philosophy; the second at least is an honourable occupation, though it tends to compliment itself, rightly, more on its techniques than its good sense. When the term 'science fiction' has been broadened to meaninglessness there is room for all, even for a rediscovery of its prime function by a responsible authorship.

Whatever helps, however little, marks an honourable attempt. Physical survival can be assured—at a price. Escape into the psychotic wards is not a satisfactory assurance of anything. It is cultural sanity that must be preserved.

ENVOI

When we get down to those brass tacks which lie strewn in the path of speculation, what have I done in my own science fiction to further the ideas in the last chapter? The honest answer is: A little, but not much. Indeed the ideas have congealed in my mind only as the later parts of the book were being written, but they had been there in essence for a long time, the symbols of discontent with a genre that claims so much and delivers so little.

My three science fiction novels have been written around that problem of aggression and violence which has now found means to wear acceptable masks even among peace-lovers and which, when forcibly suppressed (itself a confession of failure to rationalize), breaks out in more savage forms, and in these days even argues an ethical basis for terrorism and murder.

It is my conviction, rightly or wrongly, that this is the basic human problem, but I have been able to do no more than cry wolf in a voice not much heard. Fortunately the world is stocked with better and more informed intelligences who may yet be stirred into lifting their thought beyond the needs of personal fulfilment. I can only repeat T. S. Eliot's words: 'It is not enough to understand what we ought to be, unless we know what we are.'

To discover what we are beneath our pretensions and intellectualities and knee-jerk reactiveness is an urgent necessity. It would enable us at last to call our motives, aspirations, prides and self-deceptions by their right names—

and so see clearly what may be done, even on the brink of the lemming cliff.

Do I really care that this science fiction, which I find myself damning heartily for its shortcomings, could play a useful role in the society it feeds with dreams? It is, after all, only one small possibility among many, and at sixty-seven I can be fairly certain of escaping the force of the coming storm. Why should I care?

With or without reason, I do care for the future, enough to be frightened for it. After an egocentric, selfish lifetime I find, to my surprise, that I care very much what may be the shape of the world I will not see.

BIBLIOGRAPHY

NOVELS

Young Man of Talent: Cassell, London, 1959; Simon and Schuster, New York (as *Scobie*), 1959.

A Stranger and Afraid: Cassell, London, 1961.

The Cupboard Under the Stairs: Cassell, London, 1962.

A Waste of Shame: Cassell Australia, 1965.

The Lame Dog Man: Cassell Australia, 1967.

Transit of Cassidy: Nelson Australia, 1978.

Beloved Son: Faber and Faber, London, 1978; Sphere Books, London (pb), 1979; Pocket Books, New York (pb), 1979; Uitgeverij het Spectrum, Netherlands (pb), 1979.

Vaneglory: Faber and Faber, London, 1981; Sphere Books, London (pb), 1983; Uitgeverij het Spectrum, Netherlands (pb), 1982.

Yesterday's Men: Faber and Faber, London, 1983.

SHORT STORIES

'In a Petri Dish Upstairs': *Rooms of Paradise* (ed. Lee Harding), Quartet, Melbourne, 1978; *Best Science Fiction of the Year* 9 (ed. Terry Carr), Pocket Books, New York, 1980; *Portable Australian Science Fiction* (ed. Van Ikin), University of Queensland Press, St Lucia, 1982.

'A Pursuit of Miracles': *Universe* 12 (ed. Terry Carr), Doubleday, New York, 1982.

'Feedback': *Dreamworks* (ed. David King), Norstrilia Press, Melbourne, 1983.

EDITOR

The View from the Edge: A Workshop of Science Fiction Stories: Norstrilia Press, Melbourne, 1977.

ESSAYS AND ARTICLES

'Science Fiction as Literature': *The Visual Encyclopedia of Science Fiction* (ed. Brian Ash), Pan Books, London, 1977.

Four short essays on novels of Philip K. Dick: *Philip K. Dick: Electric Shepherd* (ed. Bruce Gillespie), Norstrilia Press, Melbourne, 1975.

'Frederik Pohl as a Creator of Future Societies': *The Stellar Gauge: Essays on Science Fiction* (ed. Michael J. Tolley and Kirpal Singh), Norstrilia Press, Melbourne, 1980.

'Some Unreceived Wisdom' and 'Looking at a Portrait': *Overland*, No. 87, May 1983.

Approximately two hundred review columns for *The Age*, Melbourne, plus about a hundred articles and reviews for science fiction fanzines.

INDEX

235

236